ENJOYABLE ENTERTAINMENTS

by

LILIAN M. HEATH

First Fruits Press
Wilmore, Kentucky
c2015

Enjoyable entertainments, by Lilian M. Heath.

First Fruits Press, ©2015
Previously published: Boston: United Society of Christian Endeavor, ©1913.

ISBN: 9781621713593 (print), 9781621713609 (digital)

Digital version at http://place.asburyseminary.edu/christianendeavorbooks/34/

First Fruits Press is a digital imprint of the Asbury Theological Seminary, B.L. Fisher Library. Asbury Theological Seminary is the legal owner of the material previously published by the Pentecostal Publishing Co. and reserves the right to release new editions of this material as well as new material produced by Asbury Theological Seminary. Its publications are available for noncommercial and educational uses, such as research, teaching and private study. First Fruits Press has licensed the digital version of this work under the Creative Commons Attribution Noncommercial 3.0 United States License. To view a copy of this license, visit http://creativecommons.org/licenses/by-nc/3.0/us/.

For all other uses, contact:

First Fruits Press
B.L. Fisher Library
Asbury Theological Seminary
204 N. Lexington Ave.
Wilmore, KY 40390
http://place.asburyseminary.edu/firstfruits

Heath, Lilian M.
    Enjoyable entertainments / by Lilian M. Heath.
    184 pages: illustrations; 21 cm.
    Wilmore, Ky. : First Fruits Press, ©2015.
    Reprint. Previously published: Boston: United Society of Christian Endeavor, ©1913.
    ISBN: 9781621713593 (pbk.)
    1. Amusements. 2. Sunday schools -- Exercises, recitations, etc. I. Title.
PN6120.A5 H39 2015

Cover design by Jonathan Ramsay

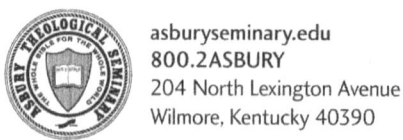
asburyseminary.edu
800.2ASBURY
204 North Lexington Avenue
Wilmore, Kentucky 40390

First Fruits Press
The Academic Open Press of Asbury Theological Seminary
204 N. Lexington Ave., Wilmore, KY 40390
859-858-2236
first.fruits@asburyseminary.edu
asbury.to/firstfruits

ENJOYABLE ENTERTAINMENTS

BY
LILIAN M. HEATH

BOSTON
UNITED SOCIETY OF CHRISTIAN ENDEAVOR
1913

COPYRIGHT, 1913, BY
UNITED SOCIETY OF CHRISTIAN ENDEAVOR

THE·PLIMPTON·PRESS
NORWOOD·MASS·U·S·A

DEDICATION

TO THE FRIENDS WHO, BY THEIR INGENUITY AND INTEREST, HAVE
CONTRIBUTED TO THE SUCCESS OF THE VARIOUS
ENTERTAINMENTS DESCRIBED, THIS BOOK
IS AFFECTIONATELY DEDICATED

CONTENTS

	PAGE
A WOODLAND APRIL JOKE	3
THE SNOW BRIGADE	11
A CRADLE-SONG CONCERT	13
THE WAKING OF THE SPRING FLOWERS	16
DICKENS BAZAAR	18
MOTHER GOOSE MARKET	19
SANTA CLAUS MOTION SONG	22
A JAPANESE CEREMONIAL TEA	25
A SIMPLE MARCH	28
DANDELION DRILL	30
AN INDIAN DRILL	34
THE BUILDING OF THE CHURCH	41
ILLUSTRATED STORIES	53
SCENES FROM "PILGRIM'S PROGRESS"	57
SUGGESTIONS IN BRIEF	72
LONGFELLOW'S DREAM	73
AN EVENING WITH TREES	79
A MUSICAL EVENING	86
GARLAND MARCH AND DRILL	89
A MILLINERY MARVEL	93
A FOREIGN EVENING	95
MRS. JARLEY'S WAXWORKS	97
MUSEUM OF VERY NATURAL HISTORY	98
LIVING CHECKERS	100
EASTER LILY DRILL	101
A SEVEN DAYS' WONDER	105
HIGH JINKS ALONG THE MILKY WAY	116
THE BEGGAR PRINCE	125
A WINDOW EVENING	134
SCENES FROM AMERICAN HISTORY	136
A SURPRISE FLOWER GARDEN	142
AN EVENING WITH THE GYPSIES	150
JUNIOR CHRISTIAN ENDEAVOR LINKS	155

To perplexed committees, arranging programmes for children's or young people's entertainments, a new book on the subject from the pen of the author of "Eighty Pleasant Evenings" will prove a boon indeed. Miss Lilian Heath in this collection repeats the success of her former volume, and renders a real service to the altruistic public.

"Enjoyable Entertainments" is the work of one sincerely interested in young people and their wellbeing, and qualified also by a wide and fortunate experience for the task. The author has here established an added claim to the gratitude of her almost world-wide audience.

FLORENCE MORSE KINGSLEY

ENJOYABLE ENTERTAINMENTS

ENJOYABLE ENTERTAINMENTS

A WOODLAND APRIL JOKE

Breeze and Leaflet Motion Song

This is especially appropriate to form part of an early spring entertainment. The platform may be without decoration and the children's dresses of the most inexpensive materials.

The Northland Breeze is represented by a boy of eleven or twelve, wearing a page's court costume with a dark mantle; the Southland Breeze, a girl of similar age, wears a cream or pale pink dress of flowing Greek outlines, with a soft pink scarf partly draped about her shoulders, partly carried in her hand as she waves it in token of Summer's approach.

Twenty to thirty small children clad from top to toe in light green, representing the Leaflets, give the motion song. Their dresses (or, if boys, Buster Brown suits) should be finished with leaf-shaped points around the bottom, with little caps, also leaf-shaped, to match; stockings and slippers (and, if girls, hair-ribbons) of the same hue, if possible; or these may be black or white, but *alike*.

The Leaflets march in to music, form a double or triple line across the platform near the front, facing the audience, and sing to the following air:

4 ENJOYABLE ENTERTAINMENTS

The Leaflets' Motion Song

1

Once I took [1] a little [1] walk,[1]
And [2] I heard [2] the strangest [2] talk
Out [3] in the woodland so charming;
For I listened [4] to the words
Of the leaflets and the birds
As they whispered [5] a secret alarming.
Then ev'ry [6] little leaflet on the fair green trees
Cried out with a shiver,[7] "I'll surely freeze,
For a message came this morning by the Northland [8] Breeze
To tell us of Winter's [9] returning!"

2

    But a robin redbreast said
    As he shook [10] his knowing head,
"How foolish to believe what they say, dears!
    For 'tis very plain to me
    'Tis an April joke, you see,
And Winter's many long [11] miles away, dears!"
Then ev'ry [12] little leaflet on the fair green trees
Said, "Oh,[13] I [13] am glad! [13] Spread the tidings, please!"
And they threw [14] a kiss to Robin as the Southland [15] Breeze
    Brought news that the Summer was coming!

3

    Then I heard [16] a tiny bell
    Echo softly down the dell —
'Twas the wee fairy telephone ringing;
    For the bluebells, you must know
    Are the wood-folks' way to show
That the very latest news they are bringing.
And ev'ry [17] little leaflet on the fair green trees
Laughed merrily out at the Northland Breeze,
Saying, "Now [18] we know the tricks you would play, you tease!"
So they telephoned back,[19] "Summer's coming!"

4

    Said [20] the Maple to the Oak,
    "Wasn't that a silly joke
When the Northland Breeze tried to fool us?"
    Said a brave Pine-Needle, too,
    "We'd [21] soon show what we could do
If old Winter should try now to rule us."

And ev'ry [22] little leaflet on the fair green trees
Went [23] nodding its head in the dancing breeze,
Till the rustle could be heard over land and seas
　As they whispered of glad Summer's coming.

5

　Then in less than half an hour
　Came [24] a roguish little shower,
And the tiny green leaflets [25] were crying,
　Till a fairy sunbeam came,
　And began a lovely game,
So that each one its tears [26] fell to drying;
Then ev'ry [27] little leaflet on the fair green trees
Said, "Come,[28] let [28] us play [28] with the birds and bees!"
And a-flutter,[29] flutter, flutter, in the changing breeze
　Went [30] the leaflets to greet Summer's coming.

The motions, made at the times indicated by the numbers in each stanza, are as follows:

FIRST STANZA

1. Take three steps forward in time to the music.
2. Three steps back into place.
3. Wave the hand and incline the head toward the right.
4. Hold one hand behind the ear and lean slightly forward in listening posture.
5. Every alternate Leaflet puts a hand up beside the lips and whispers confidentially to his or her neighbor.
6. All beat time during the whole of this line by slightly raising and lowering both hands and turning a little from side to side in time with the music.
7. Leaflets shiver and hug themselves as if cold.
8. Turn and point toward the end of the platform representing the north.
9. Leaflets raise both hands an instant as if in horrified surprise.

A WOODLAND APRIL JOKE 7

During the interlude between the first and second stanzas the Leaflets crouch shivering on the floor, while the Northland Breeze runs across the rear of the platform, entering at the north and leaving at the south end, and triumphantly waving a slip of paper like a telegram as he goes. The Leaflets then stand and resume the song.

SECOND STANZA

10. Shake the head and forefinger impressively during this and the following line.
11. Wave the hand toward the north in a long, slow, sweeping gesture.
12. Beat time as in the corresponding line in the first stanza.
13. Clap the hands three times.
14. Throw a kiss.
15. Wave the hand toward the south.

During the interlude after the second stanza the Leaflets clap their hands in glee in time to the music, while the Southland Breeze runs in, crossing the rear of the platform from south to north, waving her scarf smilingly at the Leaflets and the audience as she disappears.

THIRD STANZA

16. All are in a listening attitude again, while the ringing of one or more little bells is heard, out of sight of the audience.
17. Beat time as before.
18. Shake the forefinger toward the north.
19. Put the hand up to the mouth in imitation of a speaking-tube.

During the interlude after the third stanza the Leaflets turn partly toward the south and stand looking on while both the Northland and Southland Breezes re-enter, each from the appropriate side as at first, and almost meet in the centre at the rear of the platform, when the Northland Breeze starts to chase the Southland Breeze, who retreats a few steps and then recovers herself, and in her turn, waving her scarf, chases the Northland Breeze quite off the platform. As he runs off, he holds one corner of his mantle up to ward off the warm breeze from his opponent's scarf.

Fourth Stanza

20. Each alternate Leaflet puts an arm around the shoulder of his or her next neighbor, leaning confidentially toward that one during these three lines.
21. Shake the forefinger triumphantly.
22. Beat time as before.
23. Nod heads in time to the music all through this line.

During the interlude after the fourth stanza the Leaflets clap their hands as they did during the second interlude.

Fifth Stanza

24. Point up once, then down twice, to indicate falling drops.
25. Each Leaflet puts both hands up to the face as if crying.
26. All wipe their eyes with small handkerchiefs.
27. Beat time as before.
28. Beckon with the forefinger three times.
29. Wave a handkerchief held aloft.
30. Turn and fall into line for a march, while the music changes.

This closing march and drill may be led by the Northland and Southland Breezes, who re-enter from their respective sides, each carrying a garland of green leaves and pale pink blossoms. Each Leaflet also, on reaching a certain point near a rear corner of the platform, is supplied with a similar garland, these being used in the remainder of the march and drill. The children continue alternately marching and skipping along the lines described in the Garland March and Drill (page 89), and close by skipping off the platform.

Instead of all the Leaflets' singing the entire song the following plan may be adopted if preferred. The first stanza and its chorus may be sung by all; the second stanza by the children in the front row only, all joining in the chorus; the third stanza by those in the rear; the three lines of the Maple's comment to the Oak by alternate Leaflets, or by one child in the front row near one end; the three lines about the Pine-Needle by a child with a strong voice near the other end of the front row; and the last stanza by those in the rear, all joining in the chorus, varied as it is, each time.

Other variations may be introduced. There could be one, two, or three more characters, one child impersonating the Robin Redbreast, another the Roguish Little Shower, and still another the Fairy Sunbeam; that is, if the number of Leaflets is uneven, so that three new characters would complete an even number for the march. In this case the child representing the robin should be a little boy who can sing well, dressed entirely in red or red and brown; he should enter at the appropriate time and sing as a solo the words attributed to the robin. The Roguish Little Shower should be a jolly-looking little boy dressed as a gnome or wood-brownie, all in close-fitting gray with a long toboggan-cap and carrying a sprinkler. He should enter just at the close of the last interlude; and, when the

Leaflets mention him in their song, he should run along behind them and sprinkle them lightly with the water he is supposed to carry. The Fairy Sunbeam is a dainty little golden-haired girl all in bright yellow, with star-tipped wand and gauzy wings. The "lovely game" which she introduces would appropriately be a series of motions with her wand in time to the music, as she skips around the platform. As she approaches the rear at the north end (she should enter at the south), she waves her wand and the Northland Breeze peeps out, coming in a moment later at the same time with the Southland Breeze in time to lead the march. The Robin, Shower, and Sunbeam then fall into line with the others as the music changes.

Some may prefer this version of the last stanza:

>Now in less than half an hour
>Came a gentle little shower
>Crowning each tiny leaf with a jewel,
>Till a fairy sunbeam came,
>And began a lovely game,
>So the North quite forgot to be cruel.
>Then ev'ry, etc.

If it is given in this way, the Gentle Little Shower could be a little girl in a gray dress spangled with silver (either beads or bits of silver paper) who comes in behind the Leaflets and makes a sprinkling motion with her hands over their heads.

THE SNOW BRIGADE

A MOTION SONG FOR BOYS

ANY convenient number of small boys may take part. A sheet is spread down on the platform and securely tacked at the corners. Snowballs made of cotton are placed about, to be thrown by the boys at one another and into the audience at the time indicated. Strips of cotton hang over the edge of the platform and form little ridges and hillocks of snow, to be removed by the small shovellers. Snowflakes made of paper are sewed to the boys' caps and coats, and the sparkling "snow powder" sprinkled on clothing and floor completes the wintry scene.

TUNE, "YANKEE DOODLE"

[*The boys march in, shouldering light wooden snow-shovels*]

A jolly set of boys are we,
  And fond of fun and laughter;
But shovelling snow we like as well,
  And that is what we're after.
Yes, we're jolly, ha, ha, ha!
  No one here need doubt it;
That you may see how we can work,
  At once we'll set about it.

We place our shovels in the snow,
  [*suiting the action to the words*]
And then with rapid motion
We fling the snow this way or that,
  Just as we have a notion.

[*They cease the motions, and rest both hands on the shovels, holding the shovels directly in front of them*]
O, 'tis jolly, ha, ha, ha!
To see the soft snow flying;
And boys who've never shovelled snow
Will find it worth the trying.

[*They resume the motion of shovelling*]
See! The path is growing wide,
But now our arms are aching;
[*They lay down the shovels, and cross one arm over the other, holding them thus while they sing the next two lines*]
And while we rest them, where's the harm
In boyish frolic taking?
[*They stoop down as though picking up snow and making snowballs, throwing them, some at one another and some into the audience*]
We throw the snowballs, ha, ha, ha!
Fast they fly and faster;
Look out for broken window-panes,
Or other sad disaster.

[*They resume the shovelling*]
Now to our work we turn again;
With laugh and cheer we're greeted;
Again we lay our shovels down;
[*laying them down*]
Our work is quite completed.
That is jolly, ha, ha, ha!
And though our ears do tingle,
[*rubbing their ears or holding their hands over them*]
What care we for winter's cold
When work with play we mingle?
[*picking up the shovels and placing these on their shoulders*]

And now before we march away
  We ask you, friend and neighbor,
To save your shovelling for the boys
  Who're not afraid of labor.
We call ourselves the "Snow Brigade,"
  And this is our ambition:
To earn some pennies or some dimes
  With which to help the mission.
    [*They march out in line*]

A CRADLE-SONG CONCERT [1]

A VERY beautiful entertainment to be given by little girls from ten to fourteen years of age is an evening of cradle-songs, to the fair-haired children being given the German, Scotch, Swedish, Russian, and English parts, and to the brunettes the Italian, Mexican, French, Japanese, and Indian songs. Music and words can be found at almost any large music house, where they are easily ordered if not in stock.

Behind each nationality, as the little girls take their places, should be arranged some distinctive feature of the race or country: plaids and heather behind the Scotch lassies; a wigwam, with fire inside and imitation snow outside, for the Indian women, etc. The music also may be national to some extent in the choice of instruments: for the Scotch the bagpipes, for the Indian a tomtom or drum, for the Spanish the mandolin or guitar.

Suggestions are here given for most of the songs, cos-

[1] By courtesy of *The Interior*.

tumes, etc. Those not described are such as are easily selected in the same way.

The little Scotch girls, the tallest of the lot, should be appropriately dressed as Scotch peasants, with their great doll-babies, life-size, in their arms; and after singing

> Hush ye, hush ye, little pet ye,
> The Black Douglas shall not get ye,

they march around the platform and place themselves at the back; then come the blue-gowned German mothers, with tight braids of hair and pure white caps and aprons, their dolls hugged tightly to them as they sing the familiar song of the Fatherland, "Hush, my babe, and do not cry."

They range themselves sparsely in front of the Scotch line; and, as the music changes to "Lullaby, my pretty baby," eight Russian mammas, in magenta-hued dresses, fur-trimmed, with colored aprons and tall caps, seat themselves in small chairs as they croon to the doll-children in their arms.

The quaintly gowned Japanese types carry a fan in one hand (some of the line may alternate with paper parasols) and the doll in the other. As they chant, "Sleep, sleep on the floor; be good and slumber," they sit on the floor, while the music changes to "Slumber, for the mocking-birds are singing," and eight little Mexican mothers enter in gowns of red, green, and white, Spanish caps, spangled sashes and boleros, and, placing the huge dolls on the floor before them, clash their tambourines as they sing. This is very effective; then, as the tambourines are tucked out of sight in the gay sashes, the Italians in bright-colored gowns come forward with their dollies and, singing "Dormi, dormi, mia bambina," the Neapolitan ninna-nanna or lullaby, take their places upon one side of the platform, opposite the Mexicans.

The small French women in Norman and Breton costumes carry their babes in tiny wooden cradles, which they deposit before them and rock tenderly with one foot as they sing softly, "Sleep, sleep; my little babe must slumber."

Last of all are the tiny Indian mothers, dressed as squaws, their pappooses strapped to their backs. As they chant the weird cradle-song of the Indian, "Nic-nac-no-shin-nady," they group themselves together at an assigned spot, forming a dainty picture not soon to be forgotten. For one instant the children stand thus; then all burst into the chorus:

> Rock-a-bye, baby, on the tree-top;
> When the wind blows, the cradle will rock,

and the curtain falls or the children march out to music, in double file.

This cradle-song concert is one of the most effective of children's entertainments, and, if properly executed, can be made extremely beautiful. Sometimes the main part is followed by a second picture showing the platform arranged as a nursery, with a large number of tiny children robed alike in white night-dresses and ruffled nightcaps, a long line of sleepy heads, who, as they march from the platform in double line, sing in unison:

> Sleep, baby, sleep;
> The little stars are sheep, etc.

But it is complete without this feature and can be adapted to a larger or smaller number of children by varying the number in each group or by omitting some nationalities or adding others. If it is desired to add a group of American mothers, a very pretty song for them would be "Slumber Boat."

THE WAKING OF THE SPRING FLOWERS

THIS was given four times in the same community, never failing to delight those who witnessed it. If the platform can be covered with green, representing grass, it adds to the effect, but is not necessary. Four little girls, the smaller the better, are required. The Crocus wears a yellow dress; the Mayflower a pale pink one or thin white over a pink lining; the Violet a dress of blue; while the Rosebud, who should be the smallest of all, is clad in bright pink. The piece opens as a picture, with the Crocus standing, the other three lying asleep on the ground in various places, not all in a row, but strewn about as flowers would be, and with their faces all turned more or less in the direction of the audience.

CROCUS [confidentially, to the audience]

    I am a little Crocus, didn't you know?
    I have been sleeping down under the snow,
    But an angel thrust under my coverlet white
    This morning a long, golden finger of light,

WAKING OF THE SPRING FLOWERS

And it woke me right up; don't you think it was a pity?
But then, my new yellow dress is so pretty
That perhaps, after all, it was all for the best;
And I think it is time to wake up the rest.
  [*turning toward Mayflower*]
Mayflower, Mayflower, open your eyes!
Did you not know it was time to arise?

MAYFLOWER [*rising and coming forward, rubbing her eyes sleepily*]

Am I a Mayflower or a Bluebell?
I am so-o-o sleepy I hardly can tell;
But I am so small, and my cheeks are so pink,
That I must be a Mayflower, I rather think.
And then I sway on my slender feet,
  [*swaying a little*]
And I would not wonder if I were sweet,
And look a little bit like a star;
I guess you had better ask mamma.

CROCUS AND MAYFLOWER [*together, turning to Violet*]

Violet, Violet, don't you hear?
Wake up! Wake up! Wake up, dear!

VIOLET [*rising and coming forward*]

O, I was dreaming such lovely things!
How could you wake me? I thought I had wings
Of the prettiest blue, and a face so fair
That the children sought for me everywhere.
  [*pointing toward children in the audience*]
Why, *there* are the children!
  [*taking her dress daintily between thumb and finger*]
            And *this* is blue!
Perhaps, after all, my dream was true.

CROCUS, MAYFLOWER, AND VIOLET [*together*]
    Now we must give Rosebud a shake.
        [*running to Rosebud and shaking her gently*]
    Rosebud! Rosebud! Wake! Wake! Wake!

ROSEBUD [*coming forward, rubbing her eyes*]
    I guess I must be a little Rosebud, don't you?
    I was so sleepy I hardly knew
    When I first woke up; but my dress is pink,
    And I feel so *like* roses that I am, I think.
    If I am, I had better run, for a bee
    With a great bag of honey might fly at me!
        [*Runs quickly off*]

CROCUS, MAYFLOWER, AND VIOLET
    We, too, are so sweet, we had better go,
    For some one *might* want to pick us, you know!
        [*They also run away*]

DICKENS BAZAAR [1]

ALTHOUGH not a platform entertainment, this is included as the basis of an arrangement equally picturesque and pleasing. It will be seen to be instructive along the lines of the best literature, and a practical method when it is desired to raise money for the society or church work.

The booth should be presided over by the world-famous child characters which the pen of the English wizard drew for our lifelong pleasure, and as far as practicable should portray the surroundings which the books have given us.

    [1] By courtesy of *The Interior*.

For instance, Paul and Florence Dombey could have a booth fitted up as Captain Cuttle's shop, where shells, seaweed collections, toy ships, and anything in the line of natural-history souvenirs from Old Ocean are sold. A beautiful doll booth might be in charge of Jenny, the doll dressmaker; and Little Em'ly, in a stall made of an old boat, could serve chowder, oysters, lobster, and other seafood.

Poor Jo, the Marchioness, Smith, Little Nell, Pip, Estella, Oliver Twist, David Copperfield, Tiny Tim — these are a few from which to choose. Lovers of the great novelist will need no aid in selection.

There should be one booth devoted to the sale of Dickens's works, both singly and in sets, and another could be fitted up with small busts or statuettes of the famous writer. A pretty feature of the evening would be a procession of children dressed to represent the small folk of England in Dickens's time, and singing one or more of the Christmas carols as they used to be sung under the windows, along the streets on Christmas morning.

MOTHER GOOSE MARKET [1]

LIKE the Dickens Bazaar, this comes under the head of fairs rather than of platform entertainments. It may be given by the children either in connection with a church fair or by itself.

A large room, decorated with cartoons and gay pictures from the immortal "Mother Goose," should be filled

[1] By courtesy of *The Interior*.

with small tables, each of which is in charge of a child representing some character from the nursery rhymes.

Stray personages from the tales may stroll about the room, and will excite much merriment. It is well that these individuals should be children from twelve to fifteen years of age; and foremost of them, of course, is Dame Goose herself, with half-short blue skirt and white apron, long red cape-cloak, and high-peaked black cap with red band, a white chemisette, and green-flowered bodice and panniers. She must wear spectacles, carry a tall cane, and have a frill of muslin or lace falling around her face inside of the cap. Her stockings may be purple, with green slippers and huge buckles, and if possible, let her draw behind her a mammoth white goose on wheels.

A boy cleverly masked as a cat, with tail, whiskers, and pointed ears, and arrayed in a dress suit, will create untold fun by promenading about with a fiddle and a bow, pretending to play from time to time in imitation of "Hey, diddle, diddle."

The barber who asks every one whether or not he or she has a pig to shave, the little old woman with her petticoats cut round about, the three scornful brethren out of Spain, the witch on the broomstick, are all good characters to include; and the impersonation by two young people of the milkmaid and her questioner is most laughable.

A king in royal robes, with a crown on his head, should take the tickets or admission fees, thus representing the king "counting out his money," while the other personages from "Sing a song o' sixpence" are not far away — the sweet-toothed queen presiding over jars or combs of honey and the industrious laundry-maid, her features still intact, stationed at a table of laundry-bags and ironholders fancy and plain, clothespins, clotheslines, ironing-wax, and other laundry conveniences. Even the "four and twenty blackbirds" could be close by, not baked in a pie, but perched on gay penwipers.

Also near the entrance Mistress Mary might sell flowering plants, cut flowers, and boutonnières from her garden. At the Baby Bunting table everything for infant's wear is appropriate. Crosspatch will sell tea and coffee at her booth, which should be so arranged that one must draw the latch to enter for a social cup, and Polly who "put the kettle on" may be her partner. One unique feature at a fair of this kind was an imitation well, from which a little boy ladled up Angora kittens for customers, while over the well hung a "ding, dong bell."

"Goosey, goosey, gander" sold pretty bedroom trifles in sterling silver and worsted and glass, fit for "my lady's chamber."

Hot cross buns at one a penny, two a penny, embraced all lines of baked goods, fresh, crisp, and tempting, and not far away Jack and Jill furnished lemonade from their historic pail.

King Cole up to date should sell, not smokers' articles, but soap-bubble pipes and bowls decorated with pictures illustrating nursery rhymes. (Such dishes may be found at the large department stores, or if some member or friend of the society can paint on china, so much the better; the pipes could then be decorated to match.) The "fiddlers three" may furnish music near this table, or toy violins or candy-boxes representing that instrument may also furnish a part of King Cole's stock.

Jack Sprat and his wife have joint charge of a table with its wares, consisting of various candies, heaped luxuriantly on a huge platter; the old woman that sweeps the cobwebs from the sky may sell all kinds of brushes, sweeping-caps and aprons, dusters and dusting-cloth bags, which can be made as gay as desired; while at Bo-Peep's table all kinds of woollen articles may be displayed. Nimble Dick may sell candles, candlesticks, and shades. As the jingle of small bells attracts the visitor to a table over which is a placard marked "1 mile to Banbury Cross," its wares are seen to consist of sheet music and small musical instruments, musical toys, etc. This should be presided over by a "fine lady" perched on a large rocking-horse.

Taffy, the Welshman, sells sandwiches of every description, and the Queen of Hearts will probably assist him, as she has home-made tarts to dispose of, while for tiny customers nothing will give more delight than Jack Horner's Christmas pie of bran, from which, for a penny, each may be allowed to pull a plum in the shape of some cheap toy. The fishpond over which Simple Simon presides is also entertaining for the little ones.

It will be seen that this idea can be varied in a score of ways to make it as simple or as elaborate as desired.

SANTA CLAUS MOTION SONG

A SPECIAL favorite with the wee ones themselves, this lively little song has its decided attractions also for those that merely look and listen. It can be sung by any number of small boys and girls in their usual dress, and either with or without piano accompaniment. The simple melody is given below, to which a harmony can easily be impro-

SANTA CLAUS MOTION SONG 23

vised by the player. At the close of the song are a few hints as to appropriate motions, though such will usually suggest themselves very readily.

1. Up on the housetop the reindeer pause;
   Out jumps dear old Santa Claus,
   Down through the chimney with lots of toys
   All for the children's Christmas joys.

   Chorus
   Ho! ho! ho!
   Who wouldn't go?
   Ho! ho! ho!
   Who wouldn't go?
   Up on the housetop, click! click! click!
   Down through the chimney with good Saint Nick.

2. First are the stockings of little Nell;
   O good Santa, fill them well!
   Give her a dolly that laughs and cries,
   One that can open and shut its eyes. — *Cho.*

3. Next are the stockings of little Will;
   Isn't that a glorious fill?
   A hammer and a gimlet and a lot of tacks,
   A whistle and a whirligig and a whip that cracks! — *Cho.*

4. Papa and mamma and grandma too,
   All, I declare, have something new.
   Even the baby enjoys his part,
   Shaking his rattle, O, bless his heart! — *Cho.*

5. Come here, old Rover, are you all alone?
   Haven't they given you a single bone?
   Here's one to gladden your honest jaws;
   Now wag a "Thank you" to Santa Claus! — *Cho.*

6. Ting-a-ling-a-ling! What is this I hear?
   Have you gone for another year?
   Hurrah! hurrah! we all will cry,
   Here's a kiss; good-by, good-by! — *Cho.*

At "Up on the housetop" point up three times in rapid succession in time to the music; at each "click" snap fingers once, with hand still held aloft from the motion just preceding; at each "ho" clap hands once; at "Down through the chimney" point down three times; imitate swiftly, as each is mentioned, the motion of pounding with a hammer, screwing with a gimlet, sticking in tacks — this is done by giving three quick little jabs with the finger at the words "lot of tacks"; hold an imaginary whistle to the mouth; twirl the hands once around each other at "whirligig"; strike the hands sharply together once at "cracks"; stoop as if patting a dog and feeding him a bone; wave the hand at "Hurrah!" and throw a kiss in the last stanza.

A JAPANESE CEREMONIAL TEA [1]

OUR wide-spread American habit of hurry, fast growing into a national disease, will subside into the background in the presence of this quaint custom, which is certainly the essence of leisureliness. Its representation is somewhat in the nature of a drill, and may be accompanied by music.

Several girls should give it in Japanese costume, not forgetting the broad sash or "obi." The floor of the platform is covered with strips of Japanese matting; three or four Japanese screens are placed about, and a few flowering plants. There are no chairs. One screen divides the platform so as to show the reception-room and also the room in which the tea is to be given. Another screen is so placed that one panel of it shall form a door into a third room, hidden from view, in which the dishes, etc., are kept; this door should be precisely six steps from where the hostess is to preside over the chief ceremonies.

It is impossible to show the custom entire, as that in Japan occupies five hours; but even in the abridged form here described it can be made very characteristic if well done. Every motion must be deliberate, graceful, dignified, and sedate in the extreme.

The hostess first enters the reception-room, and, seating herself on her heels on the matting, in true Japanese fashion, awaits her guests. They enter walking, not on their feet, but on their knees. On their approach the hostess inclines her body forward in a kneeling posture, with hands rest-

[1] Based on the description in "Our Journey Around the World," by Dr. and Mrs. Francis E. Clark.

ing on the matting in front of her, and receives her guests with a series of low bows, which they return in like manner, the head touching the floor, and finally remaining in this attitude for some moments to show their great respect.

Slowly and simultaneously all rise, and the guests follow the hostess to the other apartment, where she motions them to be seated on the matting. She then turns and takes exactly six short steps to the screen panel door, opens it with three motions, using first one hand, then the other, and then the first hand again, and glides slowly out.

Presently re-entering with the same three motions in opening the door, and taking the same slow and measured six steps from it to the centre of operations, she brings in two cups; then, on another trip, a slop-bowl; then a little bamboo dipper, a bamboo whisk to stir with, a hot-water pot, and last of all a lacquer box containing the tea. Each time, on reaching the door, she must set down what she is carrying and open the door in the manner described.

When she has everything carried in, she seats herself in the presence of her guests for the first time; and, taking from her girdle a red silk napkin, she smooths and folds it with extreme care, and then dusts the top of the tea-box with it; then, unfolding the napkin with an equally elaborate grace, she lays it aside.

Next she takes the bamboo dipper carefully in both hands and places it on one of the teacups, its handle resting on the floor. After a moment's pause she again grasps the handle of the dipper and pours a small amount of water into the teacup. Into this half a teaspoonful of the powdered tea flower is put and is stirred in with the long bamboo whisk.

A JAPANESE CEREMONIAL TEA

With slow and measured tread she now approaches the first guest in the row, and with a low bow places the cup before her.

The guest first bows until she touches the matting with her forehead, then solemnly raises the cup, touching it to her brow. She then takes it in the palm of her left hand, while the right lovingly clasps it; then she must turn it half-way around, after which she raises it to her lips and drains it in three swallows. The outside of the cup must then be wiped with her thumb, while the inside is similarly wiped with her forefinger. Then it must be turned half-way around on the palm again and gently set down on the matting.

Each guest is served in the same manner and goes through exactly the same motions. The hostess then takes up the dipper, cups, etc., one by one and carries them into the further room, pacing the six steps solemnly each time, opening the door with the three motions by using both hands alternately, and finally bids her guests adieu with the same interchange of low bows as at first.

Strictly speaking, there should be a fire over which to keep the water hot, lighted with a certain number of sticks of charcoal, half of which have been painted white. But as this will usually be impracticable, there may be a small chafing-dish or alcohol lamp instead, or the fire may be omitted altogether.

A SIMPLE MARCH

```
a * * * *    * * * * b
    *   *
    *   *
    *   *
    *   *
    *   *
    *   *
    *   *
    *   *
    *   *
   FIGURE 1
```

This will admit of many variations, but will form a convenient basis. In Figure 1 the leaders pass upon the platform at opposite points, *a* and *b*, march to within two paces of each other (followed, of course, by their respective lines), then face, making a square corner, and lead the double file to the front. At this point all form in single file, the right-hand leader falling into line behind the left-hand one, etc., and pass to the rear, proceeding to the starting-point *a*.

Figure 2 shows a back-and-forth march from end to end of the platform, beginning at *a*. Care must be taken to have the lines parallel and of equal length. On reaching the front, the leader passes far enough to the left to clear the inner line which is coming forward, and thus the return is made to *a*.

FIGURE 2

A SIMPLE MARCH

```
a * 0    0 * b
  * 0    0 *
  * 0    0 *
  * 0    0 *
  * 0    0 *
  * 0    0 *
  * 0    0 *
  * 0    0 *
  * 0    0 *
    c    d
  FIGURE 3
```

Forming again in double file at the rear, the leaders march to the front of the platform, four paces apart, and halt with their lines. At a given signal the lines face inward; and, as the music recommences, those at a and b march forward between the open lines, followed in order by the rest, thus reversing the lines and changing leaders. At the points c and d the single file is again formed, the one at d passing behind the one at c, and so on to the rear at a.

```
a *   * * *   *
  *   *   *   *
  *   *   *   *
  *   *   *   *
  *   *   *   *
  * * *   * * *
```
FIGURE 4

The next part of the march repeats the second, except that the direction is from the back to the front of the platform and vice versa.

The "mainspring march" is a winding up, as the name indicates. By following the directions indicated by the arrows, there will be no difficulty in carrying it through. The circles should be far enough apart so that there need be no confusion in the unwinding.

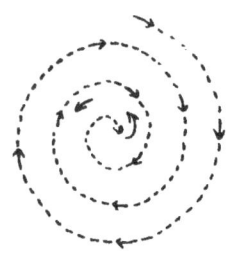
FIGURE 5

After this the line may form a semicircle or assume any other convenient shape, depending on what is to follow the march. If they are to leave the platform at once, they may form again in double file as in Figure 3 and repeat that portion of the march to where the leaders reach c and d, when, as they turn and go to the rear of the platform, they pass out at *a* and *b*, followed by their respective lines.

DANDELION DRILL

This is for any convenient number of little boys. They wear their usual suits, but over them little grass-green overcoats, all alike, made of cambric or some other inexpensive material. Each has a cane and an eyeglass (without the glass) and wears a white paper cap, closely fitting and securely fastened, over which at first is another cap made of wrapping-paper or cheesecloth covered with spangled orange crêpe paper cut into fringes. This orange-yellow cap is to be quickly exchanged at the proper time for a fluffy white wool or cotton one, leaving the plain white paper cap still on underneath.

A boy or girl recites, at intervals which will be explained, the following verses:

> There's a dandy little fellow,
>   Who dresses all in yellow,
> In yellow, with an overcoat of green,
>   With his hair all crisp and curly.
>   In the springtime, bright and early,
> A-tripping o'er the meadow he is seen.
>
> Through all the bright June weather,
>   Like a jolly little tramp,
> He wanders o'er the hillside down the road;
>   Around his yellow feather
>   The gypsy fireflies camp;
> His companions are the woodlark and the toad.

DANDELION DRILL

Spick and spandy, little dandy,
  Golden dancer in the dell!
Green and yellow, happy fellow,
  All the children love him well.

But at last this little fellow
Doffs his dandy cap of yellow,
And very feebly totters o'er the green;
  For he very old is growing,
  And with hair all white and flowing
A-nodding in the sunlight he is seen.

The little winds of morning
  Come a-flying through the grass,
And clap their hands around him in their glee;
  They shake him without warning —
  His wig falls off, alas!
And a little baldhead dandy now is he.

Oh, poor dandy! once so spandy,
  Golden dancer on the lea,
Older growing, white hair flowing,
  Baldhead dandy now is he.

But he does not need your pity,
  For in country or in city
He just takes a nap the long, cold winter through;
  And 'tis Nature's sweet contriving
  That with springtime bright reviving
Out the little fellow comes as good as new!

Spick and spandy, little dandy,
  Golden dancer in the dell!
Green and yellow, happy fellow,
  All the children love him well.

At the words "A-tripping o'er the meadow he is seen" the recitation pauses, the piano strikes up a march, and the Dandelions tiptoe daintily in, with canes down at the right side. When all are on the platform they form in one or more lines (according to number), facing the audience, and go through this brief drill with canes:

1. Hold the cane with the right hand, the end extended diagonally out to the front and the right; four counts.
2. Point the cane straight to the left, horizontally overhead; four counts.
3. Take the cane in both hands, horizontally in front, level with the shoulders; four counts.
4. Hold the cane in the left hand, level with the waist, pointing the end straight up at the left side; four counts.
5. The same as No. 1, only with the left hand, pointing diagonally front and left; four counts.
6. Hold the cane horizontal overhead, in the left hand, pointing right; four counts.
7. Hold the cane horizontal in both hands behind the head, level with the shoulders; four counts.
8. The same as No. 4, only at the right; four counts.
9. Lift the cane at the right, as if to strike; four counts.
10. Bring the cane down low in front with a sudden swish, stooping a little; four counts.
11. Point the cane with the right hand high up diagonally toward the left; four counts.
12. Hold the cane in front in both hands, with the right hand level with the right shoulder, the left hand level with the waist at the left side; four counts.
13. Hold the cane in both hands horizontally in front as low as possible without stooping; four counts.
14. Tuck the cane under the right arm; four counts.

DANDELION DRILL

15. Hold the cane down at the right side as in walking; four counts.

16. Turn, left, ready to march; four counts.

The movements of any short, simple march may now follow. When the music stops the recitation is resumed, while the Dandelions form a ring in the centre of the platform, take hold of hands, and skip around in a circle. At the words "Spick and spandy, little dandy" they let go of hands and run quickly off on tiptoe.

At the words "But at last this little fellow doffs his dandy cap of yellow" the boys reappear, now wearing the fluffy white wigs instead of the yellow ones and limping very slowly and feebly in. They are followed, as the recitation continues, by the Little Winds of Morning, an equal number of little girls dressed in white or pale pink, who come running in very fast indeed, clapping their hands in glee as they skip around the Dandelions, giving each a gentle shake and pulling off his white wig. The Dandelions then limp off the platform, as slowly as they came on. There are a few strains of music and the winds skip away, tossing the wigs about in a brief game of ball as they go.

The recitation now continues, "But he does not need your pity," etc., until, as the words are reached, "Out the little fellow comes as good as new!" the Dandelions briskly skip in, jollier than ever, wearing their yellow caps as at first. They come forward a moment and bow with a triumphant flourish of their canes, then skip out as the recitation ends.

The one who recites remains on the platform from beginning to end, stepping to one side during the pauses in the recitation.

AN INDIAN DRILL

THIS is great fun for the youngsters, and as here adapted several other good points will appear. Eleven little boys (ten little Indians and their chief) are to give the drill and exercise. If some of them happen to have the ready-made Indian play-suits now so common, those will be all right. For the rest, costumes are easily improvised. They were made as follows in one place where the drill was given:

Strips of fringe sewed down the sides of the long tan-colored trousers and around the bottoms of coats; wigs

made of rope combed out and dyed black and a bunch of turkey feathers stuck in the top; moccasins, belts, bows and arrows made of real willow, and tin tomahawks, which the tinner was easily persuaded to cut out and attach to handles. The Indians in the case referred to were in full

AN INDIAN DRILL 35

warpaint, this effect being produced by common red and blue crayons wet, by means of which the small faces were decorated for the occasion with great round splashes of red on the cheeks, and lines, half-moons, etc., of the blue.

The platform was arranged to represent a woods scene, of which trees were a main feature. The trees should be at least five or six in number; ten will be better if the platform is large enough. In the case referred to they were simulated by painted screens, but if the drill is given near the holidays, it would be both simpler and more effective to take up a collection of Christmas trees already set in boxes. They should be irregularly placed a little distance apart around near the sides of the platform, much as they would grow, leaving an open space in the middle. A wigwam in one corner might be added, but is not necessary. Place a log in the rear of the open space, long enough so that at the appropriate time nine of the boys can sit on it in a line, facing the audience.

At the start the children are all hidden behind the trees, one or two behind each. The piano begins playing the tune to which the old jingle, "One little, two little, three little Indians," etc., is usually sung, the air of which runs as follows:

and the Chief with a vigorous warwhoop jumps into view from the wigwam or from behind one of the largest trees, waving his tomahawk. After prancing around the platform while the brief tune is played once as a prelude, he stands still and motions to his comrades by whirling his tomahawk around above his head in lively time to the song itself, which now follows, being sung very distinctly to the same tune by some one not on the platform:

>One little, two little, three little Indians,
>Four little, five little, six little Indians,
>Seven little, eight little, nine little Indians,
>*Ten* little Indian boys.

Each of the ten bobs out from behind a tree just as his number, "*one* little," or "*two* little," etc., is sung, until all are out.

If the woods scene cannot be managed, the Indians may march in, singing the song themselves. When they first enter, carrying their bows and arrows, their tomahawks are stuck in their belts; the Chief now replaces his own and leads them in the following drill and march, the piano continuing the same tune to a simple accompaniment.

1. Take position in a line facing the audience near centre, holding the bow and arrows in the left hand, the ends downward, nearly touching the ground; this is during four measures or sixteen counts, constituting the first half of the tune as given. Every other boy steps four paces forward; four counts. Wave the right hand in salute to audience; four counts. Drop the bow and arrows at the feet; four counts. Place the right hand on the right shoulder, the left hand on the left shoulder, with the elbows close to the sides; four counts.

AN INDIAN DRILL

2. Arm exercises. Stretch the right arm straight out at the right side, one count; return the hand to the shoulder, one count. Stretch the left arm out in the same way, one count; return, one count. Stretch both arms out, one count; return, one count; repeat with both arms and return, two counts. Stretch the right arm straight up, one count; return, one count. Stretch the left arm up, one count; return, one count. Stretch both arms up, one count; return, one count. Repeat with both arms and return, two counts. Stretch both arms straight out at the sides, two counts; lower and slightly forward, two counts; stoop and pick up an arrow, two counts; raise the arrow with both hands to a horizontal position in front, level with the shoulders, two counts; raise the arrow, still horizontal, high above the head, two counts; hold the arrow vertical in the left hand, close to the side, two counts; hold the arrow in both hands horizontal in front, level with the shoulders, two counts; hold it in the right hand vertical, close to the side, two counts.

3. Stoop and pick up the bow, four counts; arrange the bow in the left hand and the arrow in the right ready to aim, four counts; aim diagonally out toward the left, four counts; bring the bow and arrow down low in front, four counts; aim diagonally out at the right, four counts; bring both down low in front, four counts; hold the bow and arrow in the left hand as when entering, four counts; turn, ready to march, four counts.

4. March, single file, winding in and out around the trees. Continue this during the full eight measures, or once through the tune as given.

5. The same, only running, double-quick time, still in single file.

6. The same as No. 4, only hold the bow and arrow in the right hand.

7. The same, only a prancing or galloping step, with the bow and arrow in the left hand again and the tomahawk flourished with the right hand, skipping in time to the music with the forward foot lifted well up and the knee nearly level with the waist.

38   ENJOYABLE ENTERTAINMENTS

8. Like No. 4, but only half as fast, creeping forward stealthily, stooping a little, with one hand shading the eyes as if peering at a supposed foe, with the tomahawk still in the right hand.

9. Stop marching, replace the tomahawk in the belt, have the bow in the left hand and the arrow in the right, four counts; drop on one knee, the knee nearest the audience, and make ready to aim, four counts; hold the bow and arrow out in an aiming position wherever each one happens to be, four counts; rise and slip behind the nearest tree, four counts.

10. Peep out from behind the tree cautiously, crouching as if about to spring, four counts; take the tomahawk out of the belt in the right hand, four counts; dash forward suddenly with a warwhoop to the very front of the platform, brandishing the tomahawk fiercely, four counts; remain thus in an irregular group with uplifted tomahawks while a red light is thrown on the scene, four counts.

The music stops. The boys replace their tomahawks in their belts and form in line again, still facing the audience, while the Chief, a few steps in advance, also facing the audience, recites the following, illustrated by the others leaving the line at the appropriate time, as indicated.

RECITATION BY THE CHIEF

I'll tell you a story, a tale full of woe;
But it happened, remember, a long time ago,
And you must not suppose that *our* boys would do so,
    O, no, no!

Ten brave little Indians. One began to whine,
"My lesson is too hard," and then there were nine.
[*The boy at the end of the line goes to the rear and sits down on the end of the log*]

AN INDIAN DRILL

Nine brave little Indians. One got up late,
Was cross all the morning; then there were eight.
[*The second boy also goes to the rear and sits down beside the other; and so it continues after each stanza of the recitation, till only one boy of the line is left standing*]

Eight brave little Indians on the way to heaven;
One used a naughty word; then there were seven.

Seven brave little Indians fond of jolly tricks;
One didn't play fair; then there were six.

Six brave little Indians; but, sure as you're alive,
One teased a little girl; then there were five.

Five brave little Indians playing on the shore;
One broke his promise, and then there were four.

Four brave little Indians climbing up a tree;
One robbed a bird's nest; then there were three.

Three brave little Indians paddling a canoe;
One lost his temper, and then there were two.

Two brave little Indians, with work to be done;
One said, "I do-o-on't wa-a-ant to"; then there was one.
[*Pauses a moment impressively, while the piano plays, very slowly, the last short line of the tune. The Chief then continues*]

But — here's *another* story; so wipe away your tears,
For this is how it happened in very recent years;
And when you guess 'twas *our* boys, you'll banish all your fears
     And give three cheers.
[*As this story proceeds the boys leave the log and return to the line, as they left it, one at a time, until all are in line again*]

One brave little Indian with hard work to do;
Another said, "I'll help you"; then there were *two*.

Two brave little Indians, happy as can be,
One got hurt, but only laughed; then there were *three*.

Three brave little Indians wishing there were more;
One helped a smaller boy; then there were *four*.

Four brave little Indians very much alive;
One wouldn't stone a bird; then there were *five*.

Five brave little Indians sent to feed the chicks;
One didn't stop to play; then there were *six*.

Six brave little Indians on the way to heaven;
One told the truth when it was hard; then there were *seven*.

Seven brave little Indians racing to the gate;
One kept his temper, and then there were *eight*.

Eight brave little Indians invited out to dine;
One helped the others first; then there were *nine*.

Nine brave little Indians learning to be men;
One always kept his word; then there were *ten*.

[*The music starts up again, playing the latter half of "Ten Little Indians," while the boys all take out their tomahawks. Then, when the music stops, the Chief resumes*]

So when little temptations, and bigger ones too,
Come to brave little Indians, what do they do?
Why, they practise, to gain skill and strength of the arm,
Then *scalp* the temptations before they do harm.

[*During the third line each Indian bends his right arm twice, feeling of its muscle with his left hand. At the word "scalp" each starts forward and flourishes his tomahawk fiercely once more, while the red light is again thrown on the scene, this time as a closing picture*]

If the woods scenery is omitted, however, and any lively single-file march substituted for the march among the trees, the music may strike up again at the close and the boys march out singing their song as at first, only reversed: "Ten little, nine little, eight little Indians," etc.; the last boy, just before he vanishes, turning and making a final flourish with his tomahawk toward the audience as the last line is reached, "One little Indian boy."

THE BUILDING OF THE CHURCH

By Rev. Carl H. Gramm, Reading, Penn.

Used for the first time during the Pennsylvania State convention in 1908.

Repeated at the Ohio and Michigan State conventions.

Being used by small and large societies in villages, towns, and cities.

Presented by the author to the United Society of Christian Endeavor.

I. *What is it?*

It is an exercise to illustrate the building of the kingdom or church of our Lord Jesus Christ, having for its motto, "For Christ and the church."

It can be used in connection with any church work, but especially for missions.

How is it done?

A miniature church is erected in the presence of the audience, in parts, which are brought upon the stage by little carpenters. In connection with each part there is an appropriate exercise by a reciter and a group of costumed children, who sing a song suited to each part. When the building is complete in all its parts there is a drill which also illustrates the use of the building.

The original programme is as follows:

HYMN, "Reading Juniors."

TUNE, "LET A LITTLE SUNSHINE IN"

We're the Reading Juniors, of our city loved;
That our mission is a noble one we've proved,
For we live for Christ and all that He would do,
    Lifting up His banner high.

Chorus

We're the Reading Juniors true,
Happy hearts and faces too;
And we'll live for Jesus all our whole lives through,
    Lifting up His banner high.

We're children of the great Endeavor band,
Reaching out to all the world from our dear land;
And, though young, there's much that we can do for Christ,
    Lifting up His banner high.

THE BUILDING OF THE CHURCH

And the place we have among you is not small;
We're the coming army of Endeav'rers, all;
We will act our parts with love and purpose true,
    Lifting up His banner high.

And for Christ we'll think and act and do and be;
"Doubt not, but go forward," shall our motto be,
Laying up our treasures for eternity,
    Lifting up His banner high.

PRAYER.
ADDRESS.
HYMN, "For Christ and the Church."

    "For Christ and the church" we stand,
    United heart and hand;
      Our lips His praise to speak,
      Our hands to help the weak,
      Our feet the lost to seek,
    "For Christ and the church."

Chorus

    "For Christ and the church" we stand,
    United heart and hand;
      Our lives we give, henceforth to live
    "For Christ and the church."

    "For Christ and the church" we pray,
    And labor day by day;
      With zeal and courage new
      We'll strive some work to do,
      And keep our covenant true,
    "For Christ and the church." — *Cho.*

    "For Christ and the church" we sing,
    And glad hosannas bring;

Since He hath made us free,
And promised victory,
Our motto still shall be,
"For Christ and the church." — *Cho.*

EXERCISE, The Building of the Church. Prepared by Rev. Carl H. Gramm.

RECITATION.

HYMN, "The Church's One Foundation."

Part I. Pillars ("India, O India").[1] India.
   II. Walls ("Building Every Day"). China.
   III. Windows ("The Light of the World is Jesus"). Philippine Islands.
   IV. Roof ("Dear to the Heart of the Shepherd"). Syria.
   V. Door ("My Country, 'tis of Thee"). American Indians.
   VI. Tower ("Reapers for the Harvest"). Africa.
   VII. Bell ("Fling out the Banner"). Japan.

HYMN, "Little Builders."

DRILL, by the Nations.

See heathen nations bending
Before the God we love,
And thousand hearts ascending
In gratitude above;

[1] The Ohio committee selected different hymns as follows:
   Part I. Pillars, "Where the Sacred River Flowing."
   " II. Walls, "Come over and help us."
   " IV. Roof, "Send the Light."
   " VI. Tower, "Dark Africa."
No doubt others have chosen different songs from these.

THE BUILDING OF THE CHURCH

> While sinners, now confessing,
> The gospel call obey,
> And seek the Saviour's blessing,
> A nation in a day.

MIZPAH BENEDICTION.

RECESSIONAL HYMN, "Onward, Christian Soldiers."

This can be given with many or few children; it can be easily suited to the occasion and to conditions. The expense is not great. It can be rendered in about one hour.

II. *What is necessary?*

1. Recitation, which is as follows with notes:

JUNIORS AND JUNIOR WORKERS OF OUR STATE.

Dear Friends, — We welcome you to our rally, and hope that you will receive an inspiration from it which you can take back to your society, and thus do still better work for the Master than you are now doing.

We are all engaged in one work and all have the same motto, "For Christ and the church." It was Christ's earnest desire before He left this world, after having died for the world, that the whole world should know of Him and His salvation. He said, "Go ye into all the world, and preach the gospel to every creature."

If we love Christ, we will keep His commandments, and if we are for Christ, we will spread the good news of His redemption. This can best be done through the church.

We all belong to a church and should all have a part in this great work, each one in his own church, yet all united for one Christ.

It is now our intention to build a church, and by so doing we wish to illustrate how the kingdom of God is to grow to completion on earth. Even though you see the church, yet we want you to think of the spiritual church which cannot be seen.

The building will be a very plain one, yet firmly put together; and by it we illustrate the simple but firm faith which all believers must have.

To build this church each part must sustain another and all must hold together so that the building will not fall. All believers in Christ are to work together in the spreading of God's kingdom on earth and the salvation of the world, and in so far as we are rooted in Christ can we sustain one another and help others.

The carpenters who will put the church together represent those who are especially set aside for serving the Master.

The different denominations, representing different nations, will now place the different parts of the building; this has no special significance aside from the fact that we are all united in establishing the church throughout the world.

You notice here that the foundation is already laid. We do not make our foundation; that is laid for us. The first great missionary, the apostle Paul, who was one of the first builders of the church, tells us, "For other foundation can no man lay than that is laid, which is Jesus Christ."

Song, "The Church's One Foundation."

Part I. Carpenters enter with pillars, and at the same time the first group enters.

Recite: Next you will see how the pillars are fastened into the foundation, so that they may be strengthened to hold the other parts together. The Lord said, "Him that overcometh will I make a pillar in the temple of my God." The pillars, then, represent those who have gone before and have been faithful to the Master. They are to strengthen us in all our efforts, because they prove to us what can be done if we are firmly rooted in the truth as it is in Jesus Christ.

THE BUILDING OF THE CHURCH

Song by the nation, while carpenters place the pillars. The nation takes its place on the stage.

PART II. Carpenters enter with walls, and at the same time the second group appears.

RECITE: The walls are the symbol of salvation, for we read in God's Word, "Thou shalt call thy walls salvation." Walls are a protection; and, if we do not have the walls of salvation surrounding us, we are like a city that has no walls and is in constant danger of the evil one.

Song by the nation, while the carpenters place the walls. The nation takes its place on the stage.

PART III. Carpenters enter with windows, and the third group enters.

RECITE: Windows are used to admit light into a dark place. Christ said, "I am the light of the world," and all that believe in Jesus and His followers are called "the children of light." That is why Jesus says to us, "Let your light shine before men, that they may see your good works, and glorify your Father which is in heaven."

Song by the nation, while carpenters place the windows. The nation takes its place on the stage.

PART IV. Carpenters enter with the roof, and the fourth group enters.

RECITE: The roof is an important part of the building, because it is a shelter. And the Lord is thus spoken of by David: "Thou hast been a shelter for me," and that is why we sing that hymn, "A Shelter in the Time of Storm."

Song by the nation, while carpenters place the roof. The nation takes its place on the stage.

PART V. Carpenters enter with the door, and the fifth group enters.

RECITE: Perhaps the most important part of this illustration is the door. The door is the place of entrance and admittance where the hidden treasures are shown to us. Christ said, "I am the door; by me if any man enter in, he shall be saved, and shall go in and out, and find pasture." A door is opened to us when we knock; for the Lord said, "Knock, and it shall be opened unto you." We must all remember that the heathen are knocking at the door of salvation, and we must help to open the door so that they can enter and be saved.

Song by the nation, while the carpenters place the door. The nation takes its place on the stage.

PART VI. Carpenters enter with the tower, and the sixth group enters.

RECITE: But, we ask, how can this all be done? We cannot do it alone. And the next thing we put on this building will show you how it shall be done.

The tower is a symbol of strength, and many people who know the Lord must say, "Thou hast been a strong tower from the enemy," and again, "The Lord has been my fortress, my high tower, and my deliverer, my shield, and he in whom I trust."

Song by the nation, while carpenters place the tower. The nation takes its place on the stage.

PART VII. Carpenters enter with the bell, and the seventh group enters.

RECITE: And now the last thing necessary to complete this church is the bell. The bell is to call the people to the house of God and remind them of their religious privileges. We are sent by Jesus, as were His disciples, to go and say, "The Master is come, and calleth for thee."

Song by the nation, while carpenters place the bell.

THE BUILDING OF THE CHURCH

2. Music:

For the songs see the programme above, with the footnote.

It is well to have not only a good pianist, but also an assistant who will have the music arranged so that it is all ready when it is to be used.

3. Characters:

A reciter, who explains each part.

Seven groups, of eight or four children each, who sing.

A chorus of children, as large as possible.

Four little carpenters and an older boy, who place the parts of the building.

4. Costumes:

The reciter is dressed in cap and gown.

The groups of children are dressed according to the nation they represent. These costumes are easily made by the parents of the children if assisted by a leader. There is practically no expense connected with this. Almost every church worker is familiar with the costumes worn by the nations represented.

The chorus may be dressed in white.

The carpenters should be dressed in overalls, etc.

5. The structure of the miniature church:

This is very simple, as the picture shows.

Dimensions: five feet wide, six feet long, seven feet high. (The door must be five feet in the clear, so the children can march through it.) Held together by hooks.

The parts are:

Pillars, or the front, one piece.

Walls, or the sides, two pieces, hooked to the front, with an extra piece in the back to support the end of the walls and the roof.

Windows (hung on the inside), two, one on each side.
Roof (laid on top), two pieces.
Door (hung on), one piece.
Tower (set on the roof), one piece.
Bell (put in the tower through a little opening in the back).

The cost:

Hardware	$0.60
Lumber	6.40 (use only half-inch boards)
Labor	3.12
	$10.12

The church can, perhaps, be made of canvas or paper fastened on framework. In Pennsylvania the convention committee sent the building by freight to those who wanted it. It is now used up.

Of course the exercise can be given without the structure, but it loses its effectiveness.

6. The drill:

The placing of the children on the platform is very important for the drill. After each group sings its song it marches to the rear of the stage. Thus, for instance, when the building is completed, the first nation to sing, India, will be in the rear and the last group to sing, Japan, will be in the front.

A good, cool-headed leader is necessary.

The drill has four scenes.

Scene 1. When all are thus placed, a march is played and all face the right. The leader starts to march to the right around the stage to form a circle. When the circle is complete and the leader is in the middle of the rear of the stage, he comes to the front in a straight line. In the

THE BUILDING OF THE CHURCH 51

front the children are parted, one to the right, the other to the left alternately, until the ring has been divided. When the two ends meet in the rear, they unite and come up by twos in front, where they are again parted alternately as before, this time by twos. When they meet in the rear, they unite and come up by fours in front, where they are again divided alternately by fours. When they meet in the rear, they unite and come up by eights; that is, the complete or full group is together again. When this is finished, the children are found in exactly the same position as before.

Note. Some one must be stationed in the front and the rear to see that the children part and unite properly.

Scene 2. This time all take hold of hands and hold them over their heads in an arch. The march is played and all keep step. At each eighth beat or count the front row takes a step backward and the rest a step forward, passing under the lifted arms. This is continued until all those in the rear have been in front and those in the front have been in the rear. In other words, it is repeated until the front row, Japan, has been to the rear and has come back again to the front. Thus, when this is finished, the children are again in their original positions.

Note. Time is important here, and there should be enough assistants stationed to count for the children.

Scene 3. Again all face the right; and the leader starts out, marches around the stage in a circle, and this time keeps on marching, passing inside, and thus winding them all in a spider-web or spiral drill.[1] Here all are intermingled, and the appearance of the costumes as the different nations

---

[1] This is also known as the "mainspring march." See page 29 for a diagram.

are thus blended one with another is beyond all description. The end of this is when all are again unwound, so to say, and all disappear from the sight of the audience, but always marching in proper order. As the last one disappears the leader again appears, and this time all march through the church. After having gone through the church the groups take their original positions on the stage.

Note. This takes a well-drilled leader who will not get tangled up himself.

Scene 4. Now all the costumed children kneel with bowed heads; and the children of the chorus, which should be banked in the rear of the stage, arise and sing, "See heathen nations bending." The group children remain kneeling, when suddenly the children of the chorus produce American flags, which were concealed until now, and sing "The Star-Spangled Banner." Here the entire audience rises and the climax is reached, a climax that will remain in the hearts forever.

Note. This last feature should not be printed on your programme.

Any one can readily see the deep significance of this exercise; every act is planned to teach a lesson, and there is unity and plot in it all.

General Principles to be Followed

1. Study the programme carefully, and read the explanations between the various parts which are indicated as Notes.

2. Have the groups all arranged in proper exact order on the left of the stage, behind the scenes, just as they are expected to come out to do their part, under the leadership

ILLUSTRATED STORIES

of one good director who knows the details. As soon as the group that has just finished marches to the rear, let the next be in front already, quick yet dignified and orderly in their movements.

3. The carpenters and the parts of the building should be properly arranged on the right of the stage under the direction of one good person who watches the groups as they come out. Let the boys appear with the proper part of the building, but remain standing silently with part in view of audience, while the reciter speaks. When the group sings, the part is placed. The building is to be erected well toward the rear of the stage, to leave room for the drill in front. An older boy should be stationed at the building to fit it together.

4. The reciter remains on the front of the stage all the time until the drill commences, standing in the middle when speaking and stepping to the left when there is singing.

5. There should be no announcing after the hymn "For Christ and the Church." The reciter takes his place and is the only one who speaks. The rest all work quietly, but on time.

ILLUSTRATED STORIES

A GREAT variety of beautiful, striking, and impressive scenes may be arranged based on history, poetry, stories from the Bible and from other literature, and from mission lands, both home and foreign. Costumes and accessories may often be of the simplest, for imagination can be enlisted to supply much that is lacking. When appropriate music, readings, or recitations are combined with the scenes portrayed, they can be made very interesting and effective.

All tableaux or scenes of this nature, whether moving or stationary, speaking or silent, depend chiefly for success either on the use of suitable pictures as models or on local ingenuity and experiment, and especially on the artistic taste of the local stage-manager, rather than on any written directions which can be given. Certain hints may, however, be of service.

Beginning with the Bible, the following suggestion from Amos R. Wells in *The Christian Endeavor World* is so elastic in its possibilities as to be easily extended or adapted from a simple device to make the regular meeting more impressive, to a whole evening of Bible scenes taken from certain of the Old Testament stories, from some of the parables, or from incidents in the lives of the disciples.

A Novelty for the Meeting

Curtain off a corner of the room. Put a veil of mosquito-netting back of the curtain, through which to see the tableaux. Turn down all lights except those thrown upon the tableaux. Then have the various scenes in the life of Joseph shown in a series of groups and single figures, presented rapidly, with no elaborate scenery, the attitudes mainly telling the story. After each tableau let a different Endeavorer point the moral of the scene in a few earnest sentences. — A. R. W.

A slightly different treatment, suggested by Rev. R. P. Anderson, as adapted to Intermediate societies, would be to select boys to represent the principal characters in the story of Joseph's life; let them memorize the words spoken by these characters and act out the story, including the spoken parts, the superintendent to give the connecting links. Intersperse suitable songs among the scenes.

Both arrangements can be applied to many other Bible stories. Pictures abound, which will serve as more or less exact models. Of course none of those containing Christ, however beautiful they may be, should be attempted.

There can be a dozen or more scenes taken from the life of David. Begin with The Shepherd Lad, then have Anointed by Samuel, The Musician before Saul, On the Way to Meet Goliath, The Fugitive, With Jonathan in the Field or The Parting from Jonathan, David Sparing Saul's Life at Ziph, Saul and the Witch of Endor, David the Warrior, David Made King, Mourning for Absalom, Shimei's Confession, The Invitation to Barzillai, David's Psalm of Praise, Bathsheba before the King, The Charge to Solomon.

The book of Esther has been made the subject of many representations, some of them most elaborate. From the book of Ruth one could include Naomi's attempted farewell and the well-known picture of Ruth, the Gleaner. The latter, when the occasion is suitable, might be represented by a little girl and accompanied by the song, "I am a Little Gleaner," given by the same or another child. The child Samuel in the picture, "Speak, Lord, for thy servant heareth," is also as well known as it is beautiful.

The Rescue of the Infant Moses, Rebekah at the Well, Moses Smiting the Rock, Elijah and the Fagot-Gatherer, Elijah Casting his Mantle upon Elisha, Daniel's Plea to the Steward, Daniel Interpreting the King's Dream, The Writing on the Wall, Daniel Praying with Open Windows, On the Way to the Den of Lions, King Darius in Fear for Daniel, Coming Forth from the Den of Lions — these are a few specimens of the striking scenes which may be given from the Old Testament alone.

From the New Testament we have The Shepherds and the Angels, The Journey of the Three Wise Men, The Flight into Egypt, Preaching of John the Baptist, The Fishermen Mending their Nets, The Disciples in Fear of Shipwreck, The Blind Beggar or Rise He Calleth Thee, The Rejoicing of Bartimæus, Strewing His Path with Flowers, Peter's Denial, At the Empty Tomb, Peter and John Healing the Cripple, The Angel in the Prison, and, from the parables, The Sower, The Unmerciful Creditor, Didst thou not Agree with me for a Penny? The Prodigal Son, The Wise and the Foolish Virgins, The Buried Talent, The Good Samaritan.

Try an evening of songs illustrated by Bible scenes or of Bible scenes commented on entirely by song. For example, on announcing the tableau of The Shepherds and the Angels, sing a verse of "While Shepherds Watched their Flocks by Night"; for The Blind Beggar sing "Pass Me Not" and follow it with the beautiful song, "Blind Bartimæus," by Dr. Alexander Clark and Mrs. Joseph F. Knapp, for the tableau showing Bartimæus after he has been restored to sight; for the sailors in fear of shipwreck, "Peace, Be Still!" for three of the scenes in which Daniel appears sing "Dare to Be a Daniel," "Sweet Hour of Prayer," and "The Handwriting on the Wall." Others will readily occur to mind, depending on the scenes best suited to local conditions and the particular hymn-books at hand. Often the hymn will prove so appropriate to the tableau that no other announcement need be made.

SCENES FROM "PILGRIM'S PROGRESS"

GIVEN by adults, or by young people who can do it in reverent manner, a few scenes from this quaintly serious story, portraying as it does in unmatched allegory the struggles and triumphs of a soul, can hardly fail to make a lasting impression on those who see and hear.

A good reader should be stationed near the platform. Part of the music should be merely played and part sung by the society or by a choir selected for the purpose. If a curtain which draws apart is more convenient to arrange than one which can be raised and lowered, it will serve as well; but it must move easily.

The costumes should be in the style of the seventeenth century, illustrations of which can be found in many histories, biographies, and some editions of Bunyan's book itself. The accessories here suggested may be varied according to local facilities. They should not be too elaborate, as the idea is to harmonize with the story, but not to distract attention from it.

Two light but strongly constructed removable platforms will be found a great convenience. Each should be made of the length and about one third of the width of the permanent platform, and at least two feet in height. By shifting the positions of these many varied effects can be secured.

A background of sky-blue drapery with a wide brown border at the bottom to give the general effect of sky and earth will do for most scenes. A few small trees in pots or boxes may stand against this background, their positions being varied a little for each scene. More should be added for Beulah Land.

A fence or low partition, either of pasteboard or of light wooden framework covered with canvas or heavy paper, will also serve a double or triple purpose. It should be in two sections, each three to four feet high and nearly half as long as the platform. Covered with gray or white, marked irregularly with black crayon to represent the joints of stones, it makes an excellent stone wall when caught together in the centre. With the sections separated a few feet, it makes a place for the wicket gate to be inserted in another scene.

For the wicket gate you will want first of all a framework as high as a doorway, covered like the fence, and with hooks to attach it to the fence on both sides. In the centre of this arrange a much smaller gate which will swing open, just high and wide enough for Christian to squeeze through in a slightly stooping posture. Over this small gate should be printed in large letters, "Knock, and it shall be opened unto you."

Other articles needed will be described as we come to them, but the foregoing are among the most essential.

Some thirty or more scenes could be given effectively, but with the dialogue it would make too long a programme, and would fill an entire book if described in full. I have therefore selected a few which will indicate the possibilities.

Programme

Short sketch of Bunyan's life.

Hymn, "Hark, hark, my soul! Angelic songs are swelling." First verse, with the refrain.

SCENE 1. *The Coming of Evangelist*

READER. As I walked through the wilderness of this world, I lighted on a certain place where was a den, and laid me down in that place to sleep; and as I slept, I dreamed a dream. I dreamed, and behold, I saw a man clothed with rags, standing in a certain place, a book in his hand, and a great burden upon his back.

[*Curtain opens, disclosing* CHRISTIAN *standing on one of the removable platforms near the front, reading from his book, glancing up every now and then in an agitated manner, looking now this way, now that, as though in great perplexity and distress*]

CHRISTIAN [*crying out as though unable to contain himself longer*]. What shall I do?

EVANGELIST [*coming in from the left*]. Wherefore dost thou cry?

CHRISTIAN. Sir, I perceive by the book in my hand that I am condemned to die, and after that to come to judgment, and I find that I am not willing to do the first, nor able to do the second.

EVANGELIST. If this be thy condition, why standest thou still?

CHRISTIAN. Because I know not whither to go.

READER. Then he gave him a parchment roll, and there was written within, "Fly from the wrath to come."

CHRISTIAN [*after opening and carefully examining the roll*]. Whither must I fly?

EVANGELIST [*pointing to the left*]. Do you see yonder wicket gate?

CHRISTIAN. No.

EVANGELIST. Do you see yonder shining light?

CHRISTIAN. I think I do.

EVANGELIST. Keep that light in your eye, and go up directly thereto; so shalt thou see the gate; at which, when thou knockest, it shall be told thee what thou shalt do. [*Starts out at the right, as* CHRISTIAN *starts out hurriedly at the left*]

VOICES [*calling from the right*]. Back, Christian! Turn back! Be not foolish; return to us!

CHRISTIAN [*putting his fingers in his ears and hastening his pace*]. Life! life! eternal life! [*Runs out at the left, as* EVANGELIST *goes out at the right. The curtain closes*]

Hymn, "Christian, Walk Carefully." One verse, with the refrain.

SCENE 2. *The Slough of Despond*

[*To form this, place one removable platform across the front, the other across near the rear of the main platform, leaving a space between. An ample brown covering should be thrown over the whole. The curtain opens, disclosing* CHRISTIAN *and* PLIABLE *walking slowly in from the right, on the front platform, pausing a little as they converse*]

CHRISTIAN. Come, neighbor Pliable, I am glad you are persuaded to go along with me. Had even Obstinate himself but felt what I have felt of the powers and terror of what is yet unseen, he would not thus lightly have given us the back.

PLIABLE. Come, neighbor Christian, since there are none but us two here, tell me now further what the things are, and how to be enjoyed, whither we are going.

CHRISTIAN. I can better conceive of them with my mind than speak of them with my tongue; but yet, since you are desirous to know, I will read of them in my book. There are crowns of glory to be given us, and garments that will make us shine like the sun in the firmament of heaven.

PLIABLE. This is excellent; and what else?

CHRISTIAN. There shall be no more crying, nor sorrow; for He that is owner of the place will wipe all tears from our eyes.

PLIABLE. And what company shall we have there?

CHRISTIAN [*referring occasionally to his book*]. There we shall be with seraphims and cherubims, creatures that will dazzle your eyes to look on them. There we shall see the elders with their golden crowns; there we shall see the holy virgins with their golden harps; there we shall see men that by the world were cut in pieces, burnt in flames, eaten of beasts, drowned in the seas, for the love they bare to the Lord of the place, all well, and clothed with immortality as with a garment.

PLIABLE. Well, my good companion, glad am I to hear of these things; come on, let us mend our pace. [*Both hasten,* PLIABLE *ahead*]

CHRISTIAN. I cannot go so fast as I would, by reason of this burden that is on my back.

READER. Now I saw in my dream, that just as they had ended this talk, they drew near to a very miry slough, that was in the midst of the plain; and they, being heedless [CHRISTIAN *steps suddenly off backward, as if falling, into the space behind the front raised platform*], did both fall suddenly [PLIABLE *falls likewise*] into the bog. The name of the slough was Despond. Here, therefore, they wallowed for a time, being grievously bedaubed with dirt; and Christian, because of the burden that was on his back, began to sink in the mire. [CHRISTIAN, *by crouching or kneeling, brings his head and shoulders still lower, thus seeming to sink*]

PLIABLE. Ah! neighbor Christian, where are you now?

CHRISTIAN. Truly I do not know.

PLIABLE [*angrily*]. Is this the happiness you have told me all this while of? If we have such ill speed at our first setting out, what may we expect 'twixt this and our journey's end? May I get out again with my life, you shall possess the brave country alone for me.

READER. And with that he gave a desperate struggle or two, and got out of the mire on that side of the slough which was next to his own house; so away he went, and Christian saw him no more. [PLIABLE *struggles out of the slough and goes out at the right*] Wherefore Christian was left to tumble in the Slough of Despond alone; but still he endeavored to struggle to that side of the slough that was still further from his own house, and next to the wicket gate; the which he did, but could not get out, because of the burden that was upon his back; but I beheld in my dream that a man came to him whose name was Help, and asked him,

HELP [*coming in on the rear raised platform*]. What dost thou here?

CHRISTIAN. Sir, I was bid go this way by a man called Evangelist, who directed me also to yonder gate, that I might escape the wrath to come; and, as I was going thither, I fell in here.

HELP. But why did you not look for the steps?

CHRISTIAN. Fear followed me so hard that I fled the next way, and fell in.

HELP. Give me thy hand. [*Reaches his hand to* CHRISTIAN]

READER. So he gave him his hand, and he drew him out, and set him upon sound ground, and bid him go on his way.

[CHRISTIAN *is helped up the steps in the rear and goes out at the left. The curtain closes*]

Hymn, "Just as I am, without one plea."

SCENE 3. *The Wicket Gate*

[*The curtain opens, showing* CHRISTIAN *standing at the gate, knocking repeatedly. The two raised platforms are placed side by side, slanting a little so that one end of them extends into the rear left corner, across which is placed the fence with the wicket gate*]

GOODWILL [*calling from behind the gate*]. Who is there? Whence comest thou? and what wilt thou have?

CHRISTIAN. Here is a poor burdened sinner. I come from the City of Destruction, but am going to Mount Zion, that I may be delivered from the wrath to come. I would, therefore, sir, since I am informed that by this gate is the way thither, know if you are willing to let me in.

GOODWILL. I am willing with all my heart. [*Opens the gate*]

READER. So when Christian was stepping in, the other gave him a pull.

CHRISTIAN. What means that?

[*Both men come in sight beyond the fence*].

GOODWILL. A little distance from this gate there is erected a strong castle, of which Beelzebub is the captain; from thence both he and they that are with him shoot arrows at those that come up to this gate, if haply they may die before they can enter in.

[*If an arrow can just here be projected on to the platform from the right, falling a few feet short of the gate and fence, it will add greatly to the effect*]

CHRISTIAN. I rejoice and tremble.
GOODWILL. Who directed you hither?
CHRISTIAN. Evangelist bid me come hither and knock; and he said that you, sir, would tell me what I must do.
GOODWILL. An open door is set before thee, and no man can shut it.
CHRISTIAN. Now I begin to reap the benefits of my hazards.
GOODWILL. But how is it that you came alone?
CHRISTIAN. Because none of my neighbors saw their danger as I saw mine.
GOODWILL. Did none of them follow you, to persuade you to go back?
CHRISTIAN. Yes, both Obstinate and Pliable; but, when they saw that they could not prevail, Obstinate went railing back, but Pliable came with me a little way.
GOODWILL. But why did he not come through?
CHRISTIAN. We indeed came both together until we came at the Slough of Despond, into the which we also suddenly fell. And then was my neighbor Pliable discouraged, and would not adventure further.
GOODWILL. Alas, poor man! is the celestial glory of so small esteem with him that he counteth it not worth running the hazards of a few difficulties to obtain it? But, good Christian, come a little way with me, and I will teach thee about the way thou must go. Look before thee [*pointing to the left*]; dost thou see this narrow way? *That* is the way thou must go; it was

cast up by the patriarchs, prophets, Christ, and His apostles; and it is as straight as a rule can make it. This is the way thou must go.

CHRISTIAN. Can you not help me off with this burden that is upon my back? For I cannot by any means get it off without help.

GOODWILL. As to thy burden, be content to bear it until thou comest to the place of deliverance; for there it will fall from thy back of itself. God-speed!

[CHRISTIAN *goes out at the left. The curtain closes*]

READER. Now I saw in my dream that the highway up which Christian was to go was fenced on either side with a wall, and that wall was called Salvation. Up this way, therefore, did burdened Christian run, but not without great difficulty, because of the load on his back. He ran thus till he came at a place somewhat ascending; and upon that place stood a cross, and a little below, in the bottom, a sepulchre.

SCENE 4. *The Burden Falls Off*

[*Singing, as the curtain opens, of the* refrain only, "*At the cross, at the cross, where I first saw the light.*" *The two raised platforms are placed straight across the front and centre. A large cross, apparently of wood, which need be only partly visible to the audience, should be placed at the extreme left, near the front, where* CHRISTIAN *can approach it on entering from the right; and the low partition, now used without the gate and caught together to form the wall, should be behind* CHRISTIAN *as he stands gazing at the cross, partly facing the audience*]

READER [*as* CHRISTIAN *enters*]. So I saw in my dream that just as Christian came up with the cross, his burden loosed from off his shoulders, and fell from off his back [*the burden, previously loosened, here falls off and is drawn out of sight down behind the wall*], and began to tumble, and so continued to do, till it came to the mouth of the sepulchre, where it fell in, and I saw it no more. Then was Christian glad and lightsome, and said with a merry heart,

CHRISTIAN. He hath given me rest by His sorrow, and life by His death.

READER. Then he stood still awhile to look and wonder; for it was very surprising to him that the sight of the cross should thus ease him of his burden. [*A short pause, during which there should be sung or merely played one verse of "When I survey the wondrous cross"*] Now, as he stood looking and weeping, behold three Shining Ones came to him and saluted him.

[*The three Shining Ones, impersonated by three young men, are clad in surplice-like white robes. One carries a traveller's cloak, richly embroidered, another a roll of paper*]

THREE SHINING ONES. Peace be to thee.

FIRST SHINING ONE. Thy sins be forgiven thee.

SECOND SHINING ONE. Come hither, that I may clothe thee with change of raiment.

[CHRISTIAN *steps out with him for a moment while soft music plays a few strains of "I will sing of my Redeemer"; then both reappear,* CHRISTIAN *dressed in a fresh suit and the traveller's cloak. This change can be quickly effected by his wearing the fresh suit under the ragged one, which is discarded and the cloak thrown over his shoulders; but, if preferred, the cloak may be added without other change*]

THIRD SHINING ONE. Behold, I set a mark on thy forehead [*touching* CHRISTIAN'S *forehead*]. Take thou this roll with a seal upon it; look upon it during thy journey, and give it in at the Celestial Gate.

[THE THREE SHINING ONES *go out at the right.* CHRISTIAN *goes out at the left. The curtain closes*]

Singing, "Onward, Christian Soldiers."

SCENE 5. *Farewell to the Palace Beautiful*

READER. When Christian took his leave of the Palace Beautiful, his hosts provided him with armor lest perhaps he should meet with assaults on the way. Then he began to go forward; but Discretion, Piety, Charity, and Prudence would accompany him down to the foot of the hill; for, said Prudence, "It is a hard matter for a man to go down into the Valley of Humiliation, as thou art now, and to catch no slip by the way." So he began to go down, but very warily; yet he caught a slip or two.

But now, in this Valley of Humiliation

[*The curtain opens, disclosing one or both raised platforms shifted to the rear, with two or three steps leading down to the lower part in front. Down these steps, and from right to left, walks the Pilgrim, clad in armor, accompanied by the four damsels, Discretion in gray, Prudence in brown, Piety in white, and Charity in pale blue. They leave him when half-way across the platform and go out at the right*]

READER [*continuing*]. Poor Christian was hard put to it; for he had gone but a little way before he espied a foul fiend coming over the field to meet him; his name is Apollyon. Then did Christian begin to be afraid, and to cast in his mind whether to go back or to stand his ground. But he considered again that he had no armor for his back, and therefore thought that to turn the back to him might give him greater advantage with ease to pierce him with his darts; therefore he resolved to venture and stand his ground. So he went on [*the curtain closes as* CHRISTIAN *goes out at the left*], and Apollyon met him with disdainful taunts and angry threats. A terrific battle followed, in which Christian was more than once all but worsted; but he laid hold of the sword of the Spirit, and gave his adversary such a thrust that he at last sped away.

Hymn, "Thanks be to God, who giveth us the victory." One verse. Music changes to "Saviour, lead me, lest I stray."

SCENE 6. *By-Path Meadow*

[*The raised platforms now join at the right-hand end, but separate a little, slanting away from each other toward the left. For the "stile," the fence used for the wicket gate, now fastened together as it was for the wall and placed along the front edge of the rear platform, is steadied so as to stand being clambered over, and a step or two can be placed on each side of it. A green rug nearly covers the front platform, leaving a narrow path on the edge nearest the fence. For the thunder-storm, introduce the sounds of splashing or pouring of water and rolling of barrels or moving of heavy furniture behind the scenes. The curtain opens, showing* CHRISTIAN *and* HOPEFUL *just entering on the rear platform from the right. They approach the centre, but before reaching it pause and consult*]

CHRISTIAN [*motioning toward the front platform*]. If this meadow lieth along by our wayside, let's go over into it. [*Goes closer to the fence and peers over, examining the path on the forward side, which nearly joins the fence at the point where he stands*] 'Tis according to my wish; here is the easiest going; come, good Hopeful, and let us go over.

HOPE. But how if this path should lead us out of the way?

CHRISTIAN. That's not like. Look, doth it not go along by the wayside? [*Climbs over, followed by* HOPEFUL]

READER. So Hopeful, being persuaded by his fellow, went after him over the stile. When they were gone over, and were got into the path, they found it very easy for their feet; and withal, they, looking before them, espied a man walking as they did, and his name was Vain-Confidence.

CHRISTIAN [*calling*]. Ho! friend, can you tell us whither this way leads?

VOICE [*from the left, ahead*]. To the Celestial Gate.

CHRISTIAN [*to* HOPEFUL]. Look, did not I tell you so? By this you may see we are right.

[*The curtain closes for a moment*]

READER. So they followed, and he went before them. But behold, the night came on, and it grew very dark; so that they that went behind lost the sight of him that went before.

[*The curtain reopens on the same scene, only with the lights turned very low, and the two platforms now separated as widely as space will permit*]

READER [*continuing*]. He, therefore, that went before (Vain-Confidence by name), not seeing the way before him, fell into a deep pit, which was on purpose there made by the prince of those grounds, to catch vainglorious fools withal, and was dashed to pieces with his fall.

HOPE [*to* CHRISTIAN]. Where are we now?

[*Sounds as of thunder and a pouring rain. Flash a light suddenly on and off several times, representing lightning*]

HOPE [*groaning*]. O that I had kept on my way!

CHRISTIAN. Who could have thought that this path should have led us out of the way?

HOPE. I was afraid on't at the very first, and therefore gave you that gentle caution. I would have spoken plainer, but you are older than I.

CHRISTIAN. Good brother, be not offended; I am sorry I have brought thee out of the way, and that I have put thee into such imminent danger. Pray, my brother, forgive me; I did not do it of an evil intent.

HOPE. Be comforted, my brother, for I forgive thee; and believe, too, that this shall be for our good.

CHRISTIAN. I am glad I have with me a merciful brother. But we must not stand thus; let's try to go back again.

HOPE. But, good brother, let me go before.

CHRISTIAN. No, if you please, let me go first; that, if there be any danger, I may be first therein, because by my means we are both gone out of the way.

HOPE. No; you shall not go first, for your mind being troubled may lead you out of the way again.

A Voice [*impressively*]. "Let thine heart be towards the highway, even the way that thou wentest; turn again."

[*They turn to go back at the right. The curtain closes*]

READER. But by this time the waters were greatly risen, by reason of which the way of going back was very dangerous. (Then I thought that it is easier going out of the way when we are in, than going in when we are out.) Yet they adventured to go back; but it was so dark, and the flood was so high, that in their going back they had like to have been drowned, nine or ten times. Neither could they, with all the skill they had, get again to the stile that night. Wherefore, at last, lighting under a little shelter, they sat down there until the day brake: but, being weary, they fell asleep.

[*Instrumental music, played until the next scene is ready*]

Scene 7. *Approach to Doubting Castle*

[*The two raised platforms are shoved back, a few cushions thrown over them and the whole covered with brown. If possible, have a new background for this scene, made like the stone wall, similarly marked off with black crayon, and fastened to a frame so as to be quickly adjusted, representing the stone exterior of Doubting Castle. A large, irregular-shaped piece of furniture may be also covered with gray and placed so as to form a jutting rock, which partly shelters the two weary pilgrims when they lie asleep*]

READER. Now there was not far from the place where they lay a castle called Doubting Castle, the owner whereof was Giant Despair; and it was in his grounds they now were sleeping. Wherefore he, getting up in the morning early, and walking up and down in his fields, caught Christian and Hopeful asleep in his grounds.

[*The curtain opens on the view in front of Doubting Castle, with the two pilgrims asleep under the rock.* GIANT DESPAIR *is represented by a very tall man with clothing padded to look large. He should wear a scowling mask, unless he can look sufficiently fierce without it, and carry a chain and a heavy club*]

GIANT [*in a grim and surly voice*]. What trespassers are these? Awake, you rascals! [CHRISTIAN *and* HOPEFUL *sit up*] Whence came you? and what are you doing in my grounds?

CHRISTIAN. We are pilgrims, sir, and have lost our way.

GIANT. You have this night trespassed on me, by trampling in and lying on my ground, and therefore you must go along with me.

[*Binds them with chains; they rise, looking half-dazed, and he drives them before him out at the left. The curtain closes*]

READER. Now, Giant Despair had a wife, and her name was Diffidence. So, when he was gone to bed, he told his wife what he had done; to wit, that he had taken a couple of prisoners and cast them into his dungeon for trespassing on his grounds. After taking her counsel, he first beat the prisoners without mercy, then he tried his utmost in various ways to tempt them to commit suicide; leaving them for days without food, drink, or light, showing them the bones of his former victims, and assuring them that they should never leave his domain alive. But when some days had passed, and Christian recalled that he had all this while in his bosom a key called Promise, that would unlock any door, he was amazed at his folly in remaining so long in the frightful dungeon. With this key they made good their escape, and erected a sign at the stile, warning others that should come after, lest they also fall into the hands of Giant Despair.

Hymn, "Precious promise God hath given."

READER. Now I saw in my dream that by this time the pilgrims were got over the Enchanted Ground, and entering into the country of Beulah, whose air was very sweet and pleasant; the way lying directly through it, they solaced themselves there for a season. In this country the sun shineth night and day; wherefore this was beyond the Valley of the Shadow of Death, and also out of the reach of Giant Despair, neither could they from this place so much as see Doubting Castle. Here they were within sight of the city they were going to; also here met them some of the inhabitants thereof; for in this land the shining ones commonly walked, because it was upon the borders of heaven. Drawing near to the city, they had yet a more perfect view thereof. It was builded of pearls and precious stones, also the street thereof was paved with gold. They came yet nearer and nearer, where were orchards, vineyards, and gardens, and their gates opened into the highway. Now, as they came up to these places, behold the gardener stood in the way, to whom the pilgrims said, "Whose goodly vineyards and gardens are these?" He answered, "They are the King's, and are planted here for His own delight, and also for the solace of pilgrims."

Hymn, "Beulah Land."

Scene 8. *The Land of Beulah*

[*The curtain opens on a brilliantly lighted scene with the raised platforms straight across the centre and rear, green rugs, rose-colored drapery for a background, a plentiful array of flowers and trees, and if possible a grape-arbor in the rear right corner simulated with open screens and thickly covered with representations of the fruit and vine. This corner (the rear right) is fenced off with the low partition previously used, now also thickly twined with grape-vines; and it is from this corner that the pilgrims now enter and proceed to the left*]

READER. So I saw that when they awoke, they addressed themselves to go up to the city; but the reflection of the sun upon the city (for the city was pure gold) was so extremely glorious that they could not as yet with open face behold it, but through an instrument made for that purpose. [*The pilgrims look to the left, with animated faces and gestures, through a field-glass*] So I saw that, as they went on, there met them two men in raiment that shone like gold; also their faces shone as the light.

[*Two young men approach from the left, with radiant expressions and wearing long white robes sprinkled with snow powder. They greet the pilgrims as the curtain closes*]

For the final music, have "The Holy City" either as a cornet or vocal solo.

Different music can, of course, be used in connection with any or all the scenes when preferred.

Other very effective scenes which I should have liked to include, had space permitted, are the scene with Obstinate and Pliable, with Mr. Worldly Wiseman, Evangelist's Rebuke, Asleep in the Arbor, The Porter's Lodge, Meeting Apollyon, The Valley of the Shadow, Overtaking Faithful, The Trial at Vanity Fair, The Meadow of Lilies, The Dungeon, The Delectable Mountains, Ignorance in the Crooked Lane, Caught in the Net, Meeting with Atheist, Crossing the River, The Pilgrims' Welcome Home.

SUGGESTIONS IN BRIEF

MANY fine entertainments too long to be more than hinted at here can be arranged locally, from historic events or standard literature, wherever a society can have the advantage of an experienced trainer. A very effective religious drama has been based on the life of Martin Luther. Another, taken from Sheldon's "In His Steps," will be sure to strike a sympathetic chord in the hearts of Endeavorers the country over. As to Shakespeare, Miss Helena Zachos recommends the "Pyramus and Thisbe" scene from the last act of "A Midsummer Night's Dream" as being within the powers of high-school children (which would apply to our Intermediates) when they have a good trainer. Possibly in some instances the older Endeavorers would do well with "The Tempest." I have seen an arrangement of Dickens's "Cricket on the Hearth" admirably given by young folks of Intermediate age.

Here is a list furnished by Mrs. Annie Wallace Hunt, teacher of expression in Chicago, of selections that she has used with success in her juvenile classes:

Scenes from "Little Women"; "The Rivals," James Whitcomb Riley; "Gavroche and the Children," from "Les Misérables," Hugo; ghost scene from "A House-Boat on the Styx," John Kendrick Bangs; scenes from "Mrs. Wiggs of the Cabbage Patch"; "The Littlest Girl," Richard Harding Davis; scenes from Dickens, "David Copperfield," "Martin Chuzzlewit," and others; scenes from "Ivanhoe," "Silas Marner," various Shakespeare plays, etc.; "The Pied Piper of Hamelin" (an arrangement from Browning's poem).

LONGFELLOW'S DREAM

THE general plan of this entertainment as first outlined in "Eighty Pleasant Evenings" called forth requests for a fuller description, with detailed list of characters and extracts to be read, some hints as to costumes, etc. It is to comply with these requests that I include it in extended form in my present collection. The entertainment is suited to both adults and children, and has proved remarkably effective wherever I have known it to be tried. Usually its success has led to one or more repetitions in the same community.

Thirty to forty of Longfellow's characters are selected, those most easily represented in costume and most graphically described in his poems. Arrange a platform and curtains for *tableaux vivants*, and enlist a good reader, also some one who understands artistic grouping.

When the curtain is first drawn aside it displays a young man representing Longfellow in his youth, seated in an armchair, in a reflective attitude, one hand supporting his head, and apparently lost in day-dreams. The reader then proceeds with the selected passages, while the characters described pass slowly across the platform between Longfellow and the audience. A slight pause between the readings may be introduced, but they should be nearly continuous, merely allowing each character to make the required journey before beginning to describe the next.

Characters, Costumes, and Readings

Opening scene: Longfellow as a youth, seated as already described, in a deep reverie. Let the reader begin, a moment after the curtain rises, by reading the sixth stanza of the Prelude to "Voices of the Night."

Then should follow, in turn:

1. "The Spirit of Poetry." Read from the words "And this is the sweet spirit" to "when the sun sets." Costume: flowing Grecian robe of white, rose-colored scarf or mantle; flowing hair.

2. The skipper's little daughter, from "The Wreck of the Hesperus." Read the first two stanzas. Costume: woollen dress made quite full and slightly low in the neck, in the style of the early nineteenth century, blue hood, cloak carried on the arm; blue eyes, light hair, and pink cheeks.

3. "The Reverend Teacher," from "The Children of the Lord's Supper." Read from the second stanza, beginning "Lo!

there entered" and ending with "as on moss-covered gravestone a sunbeam." Costume: plain suit, in the fashion of the early nineteenth century; white hair, benign expression.

4. "The Village Blacksmith." Read the first two stanzas. Costume: working man's clothes, sleeves rolled up.

5. "Maiden with the meek, brown eyes," from "Maidenhood." Read the first three and the last four stanzas. White dress, brown eyes, golden hair arranged in one long braid, a lily carried in the hand.

6. "Excelsior." The first two stanzas. A young man in Swiss peasant costume, a banner marked "Excelsior."

7. Benedict Bellefontaine, from "Evangeline." Read the first seven lines of the second stanza of Part the First from "Somewhat apart" to "oak-leaves."

8. "Evangeline." Read from "Fair was she" to "brown shade of her tresses" and "Down the long street she passed" to "long generations." Costume: Norman cap, peasant waist, straight blue skirt to the ankles, beads, earrings.

9. Gabriel, from "Evangeline." Read the single line, "Gabriel Lajeunesse, the son of Basil the blacksmith," then the two lines, "He was a valiant youth," etc., to "ripened thought into action." Norman peasant costume.

10. Father Le Blanc, from Section III. of Part the First of "Evangeline." Read the first five lines, from "Bent, like a laboring oar" to "wisdom supernal." Do not forget the glasses.

11. Hiawatha, from "Hiawatha," Part IV. Read the lines beginning "From his lodge" and ending "moccasins enchanted." Indian costume as there described, deerskin mittens, and moccasins.

12. Minnehaha, from "Hiawatha," Part X. Read from "Smiling answered Hiawatha" to "sunlight of my people." Costume of an Indian woman.

13. Miles Standish, from "The Courtship of Miles Standish." Read the first four lines of the poem; also the two lines beginning "Short of stature" and ending "sinews of iron." Dressed as described.

14. John Alden. Read the words, "John Alden, his friend and household companion"; also from "Fair-haired" to "Mayflower." Early colonial costume.

15. Priscilla. Between John Alden's disappearance and Priscilla's entering read from Part III. of the poem, from "Gathering still" to "the very type of Priscilla." Then, as Priscilla enters and passes, read from the same part of the poem, "She, the Puritan girl," to "rich with the wealth of her being." Puritan costume.

16. Children, from the poem of that name. Three or four children in ordinary dress. Read the last three stanzas.

17. Alice, Allegra, and Edith, from "The Children's Hour." Read the second and third stanzas. Ordinary dress.

18. "The Castle-Builder," from the poem of that name. Read the first stanza. A boy of five or six, with hair worn rather long and in ordinary dress, carries a few blocks in his hands.

19. The Landlord, from the Prelude to "Tales of a Wayside Inn." Read, beginning, "But first the Landlord will I trace" to "The Squire." Colonial costume of sober colors.

20. The Student, from the same Prelude; read from the next stanza the first ten lines, "A youth was there," to "never found the best too good." Colonial dress.

21. "A young Sicilian." See the next stanza. Read from "A young Sicilian, too, was there" to "like a swallow's wings." Dark complexion, mustache as described.

22. The Spanish Jew. Read from the next stanza "A Spanish Jew from Alicant" to "tumbling cataract of his beard"; also from "His eyes seemed gazing" to "Jewish maidens dance." Appearance as described.

23. The Theologian. See the next stanza. Read the stanza entire. Dressed like a minister.

24. The Musician. Read from "Last, the Musician" to "Painted by Raphael, he seemed." Light hair, blue eyes, tall, etc., as described, carrying a violin.

25. Paul Revere, from "Paul Revere's Ride." Read the three lines from "Meanwhile, impatient to mount and ride" to "walked Paul Revere." Colonial dress, boots and spurs.

26. Monna Giovanna and her bosom friend. Read from "The Falcon of Ser Federigo," beginning "Two lovely ladies" to "their errand and its end." Dressed in cloak and hood; in one the hood thrown back as described, showing abundant fair hair.

27. Robert of Sicily, from "King Robert of Sicily." Read the first six lines. Do not attempt the retinue. Italian court costume of rich colors.

28. The Squire, from "The Birds of Killingworth." Read the sixth stanza entire. Costume of an English squire, pompous manner.

29. The Parson. Read the next stanza entire. Appearance as described.

30. The Preceptor. Read the next stanza entire.

31. The Deacon. Read the next stanza. A large, elderly man in black, with voluminous white neckcloth, looking very wise, and walking slowly.

32. Almira, from the last stanza of the same poem. Read from "It was the fair Almira's wedding-day" to the end. Bridal costume, with veil.

33. The cobbler, from "The Cobbler of Hagenau." Read from the second stanza, from "A cobbler" to "let the next world drift." Costume of the German peasant class. Gesticulates as if arguing as he walks.

34. Mistress Stavers, from "Lady Wentworth." Read the first four lines. Costume in the style of the eighteenth century, full skirt, etc.

35. Governor Wentworth, from the same poem. Read from "A portly person with three-cornered hat" to "much at ease." Costume as described, with ruffled shirt, powdered cue, etc.

36. Martha Hilton, from the same poem. Read from "Can this be Martha Hilton?" to "all her majesty." Dressed in the English style of the eighteenth century.

37. Charlemagne, from the poem of that name. Read from "And Charlemagne appeared" to "sword invincible." In full armor.

38. Emma, from "Emma and Eginhard." Read from "The lovely Princess Emma" to "beautiful as May." Antique Saxon costume.

39. Brother Anthony, from "The Monk of Casal Maggiore." Read the entire stanza beginning "The first was Brother Anthony." Costume of a monk.

40. Brother Timothy. Read the next stanza. Similar costume to Brother Anthony's.

When all have passed, the curtain is drawn and music fills the interval while the characters are being grouped for the final tableau. This, when well arranged, is very striking and beautiful. It represents Longfellow as an old man, seated in the same armchair, with the creations of his fancy grouped about him and the Spirit of Poetry in the act of crowning him with a wreath of laurels. The children are nearest the poet, playing almost at his feet, while the others are standing, grouped as their various heights and costumes require for the best effect. The platform must of course be a large one. Gauze stretched across the front and a red light burned during the tableau add to its beauty and effect; also the singing, in chorus or as a solo, from behind the scenes, of a verse lauding the poet and speeding the Spirit of Poetry in her mission. Softly played instrumental music may be substituted.

AN EVENING WITH TREES

In a programme of this kind Endeavorers of all ages can unite. Arrange the platform to represent a woods scene, with green floor-covering; potted palms and other growing trees banked with moss; leafy branches, real or simulated, fastened up over doors and windows; and the pictures, if any, framed in leaves or decked with branches also. It is not a bad idea to make the occasion a plea for more intelligent treatment of our nation's trees. This feature will not need to detract from the entertaining character of the evening. The programme should include music, recitations, and a number of short original papers or addresses. The Juniors may help by giving some or all of the recitations and by an appropriate motion song or drill.

Early in the evening have a short address by a good speaker, which will furnish the key-note of what is to follow. Let him explain the causes and results of a national timber famine and mention some of the best ways of encouraging the protection of trees already growing and the planting of new ones.

Follow or precede the address with this poem, which may be given by a Junior as a recitation:

Forest Song

A song for the beautiful trees!
A song for the forest grand,
The garden of God's own land,
The pride of His centuries.

Hurrah for the kingly oak,
    For the maple, the sylvan queen,
For the lords of the emerald cloak,
    For the ladies in living green!

For the beautiful trees a song,
    The peers of a glorious realm,
    The linden, the ash, and the elm,
The poplar stately and strong.
Hurrah for the beech-tree trim,
    For the hickory stanch at core,
For the locust thorny and grim,
    For the silvery sycamore!

A song for the palm, the pine,
    And for every tree that grows
    From the desolate zone of snows
To the zone of the burning line.
Hurrah for the warders proud
    Of the mountain-side and vale,
That challenge the thunder-cloud,
    And buffet the stormy gale!

A song for the forest aisled
    With its Gothic roof sublime,
    The solemn temple of time,
Where man becometh a child,
As he lists to the anthem-roll
    Of the wind in the solitude,
The hymn which telleth his soul
    That God is the voice of the wood.

So long as the rivers flow,
    So long as the mountains rise,
    May the forest sing to the skies,
And shelter the earth below.

AN EVENING WITH TREES

> Hurrah for the beautiful trees!
> Hurrah for the forest grand,
> The pride of His centuries,
> The garden of God's own land!
> — W. H. VENABLE

The historic interest attached to certain trees will help to deepen the impression thus far made. Here is a list of topics from which several may be chosen for special study and short original papers:

1. The Willow-Tree of Babylon.
2. The Cedars of Mt. Lebanon.
3. The Banian-Tree of India.
4. The Baobab-Tree of the Cape Verde Islands.
5. The Chestnut-Tree of Mt. Etna.
6. The Walnut-Tree of Balaklava.
7. The Cypress-Tree of Montezuma.
8. Shakespeare's Mulberry-Tree.
9. Peter Stuyvesant's Pear-Tree.
10. Pope's Willow.
11. The Treaty Elm of Philadelphia.
12. The Charter Oak of Hartford.
13. The Liberty Elm at Boston.
14. Washington's Elm at Cambridge.
15. Burgoyne's Elm.
16. The Linden-Tree of Neustadt.
17. The Hamilton Trees of New York.
18. The Tree from Napoleon's Grave.
19. The Carey Tree.
20. The Apple-Tree of Appomattox.

Intersperse the papers with more recitations, music, choice readings, and perhaps a quotation exercise. A good reader might give from Rev. William A. Quayle's "In God's Out-of-Doors" some extracts from his delightful chapter on "Winter Trees"; also the single paragraph descriptive of the wild crab-tree, toward the last of his chapter on "My Farm" (page 219 in my copy, edition of 1902). These will be a revelation to many. So, also, in a different way would be the article by George Ethelbert Walsh on "Making Trees to Order," telling of the curious artificial training of trees in Japan, and other related facts. This is to be found in *The Christian Endeavor World* of February 24, 1910, while in the issue of April 1, 1909, is an article on forestry that will be well worth looking up in preparing for the evening, also a short sketch of Pinchot and his work. In the *National Geographic Magazine* of July, 1909, are two articles on the remarkable eucalyptus of California, "the tallest tree that grows," further facts concerning which may be obtained from the Forestry Service and other specialists in that State. Some extracts from one of the numerous accounts of Luther Burbank's work in its relation to trees would be interesting. *The Youth's Companion* early in 1910 published a series of graphic sketches of the life of a forest ranger. There will be no lack of such material, once the committee is thoroughly interested in looking up the subject.

The following poem may be recited by five Juniors, each taking one stanza:

PLANT A TREE

He who plants a tree
Plants a hope.
Rootlets up through fibres blindly grope;
Leaves unfold into horizons free.

AN EVENING WITH TREES

      So man's life must climb
      From the clods of time
      Unto heavens sublime.
Canst thou prophesy, thou little tree,
What the glory of thy boughs shall be?

      He who plants a tree
        Plants a joy,
Plants a comfort that will never cloy,
Every day a fresh reality,
        Beautiful and strong,
        To whose shelter throng
        Creatures blithe with song.
If thou couldst but know, thou happy tree,
Of the bliss that shall inhabit thee!

      He who plants a tree,
      He plants peace.
Under its green curtains jargons cease,
Leaf and zephyr murmur soothingly;
        Shadows soft with sleep
        Down tired eyelids creep,
        Balm of slumber deep;
Never hast thou dreamed, thou blessed tree,
Of the benediction thou shalt be.

      He who plants a tree,
      He plants youth,
Vigor won for centuries in sooth;
Life of time, that hints eternity!
        Boughs their strength uprear;
        New shoots every year
        On old growths appear.
Thou shalt teach the ages, sturdy tree,
Youth of soul is immortality.

He who plants a tree,
    He plants love,
Tents of coolness spreading out above
Wayfarers he may not live to see.
    Gifts that grow are best;
    Hands that bless are blest;
    Plant; life does the rest!
Heaven and earth help him who plants a tree,
And his work its own reward shall be.
                  — LUCY LARCOM

And an Intermediate or another Junior might give this one:

THE OAK-TREE

Sing for the oak-tree, the monarch of the wood!
Sing for the oak-tree that groweth green and good,
That groweth broad and branching within the forest shade,
That groweth now and still shall grow when we are lowly laid.

The oak-tree was an acorn once and fell upon the earth,
And sun and shower nourished it and gave the oak-tree birth;
The little sprouting oak-tree, two leaves it had at first,
Till sun and shower nourished it; then out the branches burst.

The winds came and the rain fell; the gusty tempest blew;
All, all, were friends to the oak-tree, and stronger yet it grew.
The boy that saw the acorn fall, he feeble grew and gray;
But the oak was still a thriving tree and strengthened every day.

Four centuries grows the oak-tree, nor does its verdure fail;
Its heart is like the ironwood, its bark like plaited mail.
Now cut us down the oak-tree, the monarch of the wood,
And of its timber stout and strong we'll build a vessel good.

AN EVENING WITH TREES

The oak-tree of the forest both east and west shall fly,
And the blessings of a thousand lands upon our ship shall lie.
She shall not be a man-of-war, nor a pirate shall she be,
But a noble Christian merchant ship, to sail upon the sea.
— MARY HOWITT

For the drill let the smaller Juniors give the little Breeze and Leaflet Motion Song, full directions for which are given elsewhere in these pages under the title of "A Woodland April Joke." If the programme is a long one, the Garland March and Drill arranged to be given following this motion song may be omitted.

Here are some quotations which may be used if desired, either as a recitation exercise or written on dainty souvenir cards appropriately illustrated and given out as the people are leaving:

There is, after all, no house like God's out-of-door. — *Robert Louis Stevenson.*

Nature is the volume of which God is the author. — *Harvey.*

The earth is full of the goodness of the Lord. — *Ps. 33: 5.*

He causeth the grass to grow for the cattle and herb for the service of man; that he may bring forth food out of the earth. — *Ps. 104:14.*

And the leaves of the tree were for the healing of the nations. — *Rev. 22: 2.*

A man who plants a tree and cares for it has added at least his mite to God's creation. — *Lucy Larcom.*

He who plants an oak looks forward to future ages, and plants for posterity. — *Irving.*

He shall be like a tree planted by the rivers of water, that bringeth forth his fruit in his season; his leaf also shall not wither; and whatsoever he doeth shall prosper. — *Ps. 1: 3.*

The man who builds does work which begins to decay as soon as he has done, but the work of the man who plants trees grows better and better year after year, for generations.

Others of a similar nature are not hard to find.

A MUSICAL EVENING

SUITABLY grouped and well rendered, the best of the old-time favorites in song will seldom fail to make an enjoyable evening programme. This one, used by the society at Plymouth, Wis., is excellent in itself and will suggest others.

Such sweet compulsion doth in music lie

Doxology .... AUDIENCE
Musical Quotations
Lullabies
    Luther's Cradle Song
              EIGHT GIRLS FROM THE PRIMARY DEPARTMENT
    Sweet and Low .. .. SOLO
Songs of Childhood and Youth
    The Old Oaken Bucket . ... AUDIENCE
    Little Orphant Annie ... . SOLO
    Far Away...... .... MALE QUARTETTE
Songs of War
    Onward, Christian Soldiers .... AUDIENCE
    The Sword of Bunker Hill .... SOLO
Songs of the Heart
    In the Gloaming
    We'd Better Bide a Wee   ... . SOLOS
    Blue Bells of Scotland . . .. SEVEN GIRLS
    Guitar solo and Annie Laurie solo

National Songs
   The Battle-Hymn of the Republic. Its Story   READER
   The Maple-Leaf Forever }
   The Watch on the Rhine }   SOLO AND TRIO
   America .... AUDIENCE
Favorite Hymns
   Sun of My Soul }
   Nearer, My God, to Thee } .... AUDIENCE
   Rock of Ages }
Songs of the South
   Old Black Joe .... ORGAN SOLO
   The Suwanee River. .... LADIES' QUARTETTE
Mizpah Songs
   Auld Lang Syne }
   Home, Sweet Home } .... AUDIENCE
   Good Night .... DUET

These are songs which will be found in nearly every community. If any are lacking or it is desired to vary the programme, here is a list of others which might be fitted into the above or similar groups to carry out the idea.

Under the head of Songs of Childhood and Youth there is Backward, Turn Backward, O Time, in thy Flight; under Songs of the South there are Dixie and My Old Kentucky Home; while among Folk Songs of Other Lands may be mentioned Lorelei, Killarney, Kathleen Mavourneen, Canadian Boat Song, How Can I Leave Thee? (Thuringian folk song), Robin Adair, Comin' through the Rye, O Wert thou in the Cauld Blast.

In Songs of Sentiment there are Love's Old Sweet Song; Flow Gently, Sweet Afton; Maid of Athens, The Danube River, Juanita, In the Starlight, Shells of Ocean, Stilly Night (using the words adapted by C. W. B. from

Longfellow's Venetian Gondoliers, and music by Haydn), The Lost Chord, The Arrow and the Song, The Bridge, The Brook, and in a lighter vein Katy's Letter; No, Sir! and The Bend in the River.

If songs in German are wanted, Heiden Röslein, Deutschland über Alles, Wandrer's Nachtlied, Der Gute Kamerad, Du, du liegst mir im Herzen, and Du bist wie eine Blume (Heine's words, Schubert's music) will be found a good list.

Among College Songs there are Fair Harvard, Ivy Song (Yale), At Wellesley, Alma Mater (Cornell), Alma Mater (University of Chicago), Alma Mater (Yale), Gaudeamus Igitur, Evening Song at Cornell, Gayly the Troubadour, Hüttelein, and Aunt Dinah's Quilting Party.

Under Songs of War may be placed The Soldier's Farewell, Marching through Georgia, The Battle-Cry of Freedom;. Tramp, Tramp, Tramp, the Boys are Marching; Maryland, my Maryland; Rally Round the Flag, Boys; and Tenting on the Old Camp-Ground; while in the list of National Songs of our own land are Thanksgiving Hymn; Sail on, thou Ship of State; The Flag of our Union Forever, Keller's American Hymn, with Oliver Wendell Holmes's words, besides, of course, Columbia, the Gem of the Ocean; Hail, Columbia; and The Star-Spangled Banner.

A group of National Songs of Other Lands would include Rule, Britannia; Scots Wha Hae wi' Wallace Bled, La Marseillaise, Men of Harlech, The Harp that Once through Tara's Halls, the Swedish Dear Land of my Fathers, the Portuguese Hymn (Adeste Fideles), The Watch on the Rhine, Russian National Hymn, Austrian National Hymn, and Tyrolese Maiden's Song.

In Favorite Hymns or Sacred Songs some good alternative selections are Rocked in the Cradle of the Deep; Lead,

Kindly Light; Guide me, O Thou Great Jehovah; Jesus, Lover of my Soul; and Abide with Me.

Make a specialty of inviting the older people of the community to such an evening's entertainment. They will be sure to enjoy it.

GARLAND MARCH AND DRILL

WHILE this is simpler than many would suppose, yet the waving and crossing of the flower garlands in their varied positions produces an indescribably pretty effect. The exercise, for the main idea of which the compiler is indebted to Imogen A. Storey, is to be given by an even number of children, dressed either in white or in light green as described in "A Woodland April Joke." The garlands, of green leaves almost hidden by white or pale pink blossoms, can be made of paper. Their length should be nearly uniform and sufficient to permit freedom of motion.

The platform may be either decorated to represent a woods scene or left entirely without decoration. The floor should be marked off as shown in the diagrams to prevent mistakes in marching. Colored crayons may be used for this purpose, a different color for each distinct part of the march.

At a given signal the children, in two lines, skip in from the rear at the points shown, with garlands held in both hands, their arms down at the side. When the leaders reach the lines R and L in Diagram A, they turn to the front and change from the skip step to this fancy step, following lines R and L.

Extend the inside foot (the foot toward the partner) and touch the toe to floor, raise the inside arm diagonally up inside, with the outside arm across the body, first count; place the foot flat on the floor and bring the rear foot beside it, with arms straight forward to front and then straight beside the head, second count.

Repeat this to the opposite side and continue alternating until the front line is reached, when the skip step is resumed. They follow lines shown by arrows and come down lines R and L from the rear in B, with the same fancy step. They begin the fancy step on the command, "Fancy

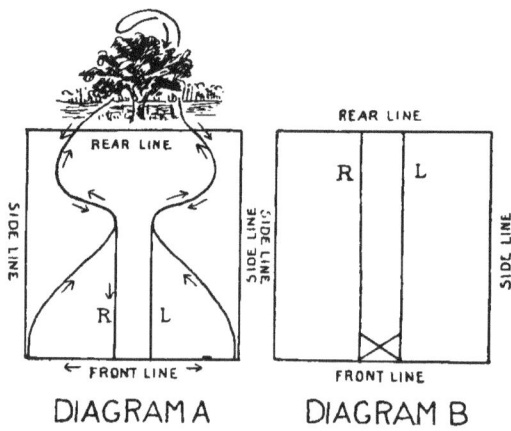

DIAGRAM A   DIAGRAM B

step, march!" from a director stationed near. "Fancy step," being the preparatory command, should be given some time before the executive command "March!" The skip step should begin to slow up on the first command so that they change smoothly in the fancy step on the command "March!"

On reaching the front line in B they turn by twos, the first couple turning to the right on the front line and the next to the left; they continue alternating in this manner and continue touch step with the inside arm held up in the same position as in the previous fancy step, only grasping the partner's hand.

When the first couples reach the cross line (F. S. in C) the director gives the command "Change!" They let go hands; and, as the outside foot is pointed to the floor, the arms are reversed, third count; hold, fourth count (the touch step is the same as before); repeat the same to the inside, fifth and sixth counts; repeat the same to the outside, seventh and eighth counts. When the first couple

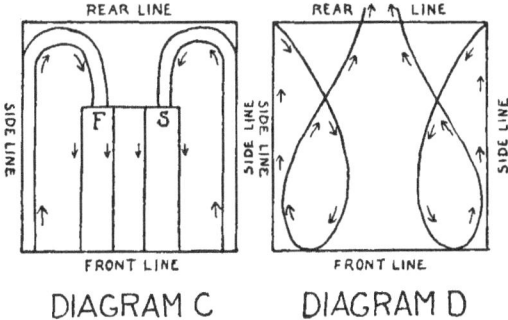

DIAGRAM C   DIAGRAM D

reach the front line the director gives command "Company, halt!" All should halt at the same time, keeping the regulation distance of a little more than arm's length from the one in front, which should be retained all through the drill.

After they have halted and brought their heels together this series of exercises is begun:

I

Those on the centre lines turn back to back. Those on the outside lines turn facing the centre. All turn together on the command from the director, "Face! March!"

All charge forward with the right foot, both arms straight forward shoulder-high, first count; let go the right ends of the garlands, second count; grasp the end of the partner's garland in the left hand, third count; bring the forward foot back beside the rear foot, straightening the knee and with the arms down at the side, fourth count.

II

Arms toward the rear of the stage straight forward and beside the head, first count; reverse arms, second count; reverse, third count; arms down at the side, fourth count.

III

All right arms up shoulder-high to the front and beside the head, first count; reverse position, second count; reverse, third count; all arms down at the side, fourth count.

IV

All left arms straight forward and beside the head, first to fourth counts.

V

Repeat II, first to fourth counts, with arms toward the front of the stage.

VI

All arms toward the rear of the stage straight beside the head as before; all arms toward the front of the stage shoulder-high at the side, first count; reverse, second count; reverse, third count; arms down at the side, fourth count.

Repeat beginning opposite arms, first to fourth counts.

VII

Both arms shoulder-high to the front and charge straight forward with the right foot, first count; let go partner's garland, second count; grasp the end of one's own garland, third count; bring the heels together and the arms down at the side, fourth count.

Arms straight beside the head, signal. Drop the garland around the neck as a boa and place the hands on the hips, second signal. Turn facing the front, third signal. Command from the director, "Company, forward, march!" They march, turning right and left by twos on reaching the front line. On reaching the rear line each grasps his partner's hand, keeping the outside hand on the hip, and resumes the skip step. They follow the lines as shown in D and go out by twos.

A MILLINERY MARVEL

THIS has been given very successfully without a platform; but if one is used, it should be a large and rather low one, so as to avoid crowding and give the audience a chance to move about and inspect the first part of the "marvel" at close range.

The main entertainment is in two parts; first, a hat-trimming contest, lasting perhaps three-quarters of an hour, in which all the milliners are men; second, a grand procession of dames and damsels wearing the finished products while the judges take notes on the particular pieces of handiwork that reflect most credit on the artists who produced them.

Each lady brings with her an untrimmed hat rescued from its oblivion and a supply of trimmings and sewing materials. In one contest of this kind, in Westerleigh, N. Y., I believe each lady also engaged her man milliner in advance; but that is immaterial, as the trade is learned with surprising quickness. Judges were appointed at the beginning of the evening; the prize offer was explained, and the milliners were then set to work in a long row behind the work-tables, each having one hat to trim in the time allotted. Each milliner was left entirely free to use his own taste; he might fasten the trimmings on with pins, needle and thread, hammer and tacks, or glue, if he so desired; but trim that hat he must, and that without feminine assistance. It would have been pathetic, had it not been irresistibly funny, to see the heroic attempts of the milliners to rise to the occasion, their imploring questions as to "which was the front of the thing" bringing them no relief or information.

When the time was up, the newly trimmed hats were restored to their original owners, a march was played, and the procession of millinery which followed was truly a marvel. The ladies passed and repassed several times, that the judges might have ample opportunity to view the results achieved.

Refreshments were served during a social half-hour while the final decisions were being reached. Then the prizes were awarded with great ceremony, one to the man milliner who had, in the judgment of the committee, produced the most beautiful and artistic hat; the second to the man milliner whose work had proved the most becoming, and the third to the one who had produced the most comical effect.

On this occasion the first and second prizes were a gorgeous bouquet and a silver thimble, and the third was a doll's hat, which was worn by its proud recipient as a boutonnière for the rest of the evening.

Placards decorating the improvised millinery shop may read "Latest Styles from Paris," "None but Expert Work Done Here," "Every Hat Unique," "Great Bargains! Two-dollar Hats for One Dollar and Ninety-nine Cents!" etc. The milliners will probably be grateful if some are added reading, "Danger! Keep Off!" "Do Not Talk to the Milliner," "Please do Not Shoot," and similar appeals and cautions.

Of course the number of ladies bringing hats must correspond to the number of milliners to be employed. About twenty milliners is a good number, though anywhere from a dozen upwards will answer. The audience will enjoy the occasion, whether they are active participants in the chief part of the programme or not.

A FOREIGN EVENING

The Christian Endeavor society of Niagara Falls, N. Y., through its missionary committee, gave a "foreign evening" arranged as follows: To each of the seven members of the committee was assigned a foreign country on which he or she was to write a ten-minute paper. Each committeeman was for the time being to be a native of the country thus described, and was to tell of the home life, the life of childhood, the educational and religious training, and some of the striking differences between the manners, customs, and religion of his country and those of America. The papers were to be committed to memory and given without any reference whatever to notes.

Those taking part were to dress in the costume of the country they represented and, if possible, to exhibit curios of that country. One girl was to represent a child widow from India and to tell what such widows endure. Women from Persia and Turkey were to tell about the position of woman in those countries. An African from the Congo would tell of the savage life and superstitious beliefs of his people. There was to be a Chinaman, pigtail and all, and an Eskimo from Alaska.

The plan, as will be seen, presents many opportunities for the bringing out of local talent, while its power to awaken a general interest is increased through the practice of original research and of thus giving original expression to the facts learned. In Miss Ruth Elsheimer's description of the thorough preparation being made by their committee she adds:

"From the United Society of Christian Endeavor we have secured 'Music from Foreign Fields,' and although some of the selections are foreign, both in words and music, we are going to sing them. The audience will not be critical of our Chinese or Japanese. We also obtained from the United Society the little ten-cent booklets descriptive of the various mission countries. The costumes will be neither expensive nor difficult to make."

MRS. JARLEY'S WAXWORKS

At a bright rally held in St. Paul, Minn., the ladies of the city Christian Endeavor union gave a very clever and successful presentation of "Mrs. Jarley's Waxworks," with Miss Lucy Gundlach, former secretary of the Minnesota Christian Endeavor Union, impersonating Mrs. Jarley. The occasion is described by one of the state officers, Clara Lilian Lewis, as follows:

Mrs. Jarley had named her wonderful collection "The Convention Committee." On being unveiled the figures presented a striking likeness to the chairmen of the 1909 Convention committee. They were life-size, and so extraordinarily lifelike that one almost expected to hear a sneeze as each face was carefully dusted with a feather duster.

Mrs. Jarley's information regarding the various figures was interesting. When a very realistic likeness of Minnesota's field secretary was unveiled, Mrs. Jarley said:

> This, dear friends, is the "Howell" we made
> To get the great Convention,
> A mighty Howell and long drawn out,
> To win the "Shaw's" attention.
> Now as we set ourselves to work
> For the great C. E. Convention,
> We'll keep this "Howell" a-going yet,
> To win the world's attention.

As her assistant unveiled the figure placarded Manager, Mrs. Jarley explained:

98   ENJOYABLE ENTERTAINMENTS

>   This is the manager, J. Powell Moore,
>   The most important man on the floor.
>   He cheers the others into line,
>   To boom the Convention of 1909.

Each figure was also able to speak for itself upon being wound up. The Manager responded with "Come to order," the Treasurer with "Present bill." The figure bearing the name of the Information Committee gave the encouraging response, "Ask me," while the Entertainment chairman's figure made the enlightening remark, "One dollar fifty per day." The figure placarded Reception smiled as it exclaimed, "Welcome!" As the last figure in the collection, representing Press and Publicity, was exhibited it called out: "Paper! Paper! Buy a paper!"

No round of applause was ever more expressive than the hearty and spontaneous way in which the State song was taken up by the Endeavorers as the curtain fell.

MUSEUM OF VERY NATURAL HISTORY

FOR a rally, anniversary or business meeting, and social combined, this feature, if well handled, can be made extremely entertaining. At the rear of the platform hang two curtains; one from above the heads down to a level with the waists of persons standing in front of it; then, from a board fastened across for a shelf a little below the persons' shoulders, have a second curtain hanging from the front edge of the shelf to the floor, so that a row of persons standing in front of the upper curtain but behind

MUSEUM OF VERY NATURAL HISTORY 99

the lower one would be concealed except above the waist. Make of tissue-paper a large owl's head for each of these persons to slip over his own head. They are not at all difficult to make so that they look natural at a little distance. Tissue-paper owls' wings may also be made and fastened to the shoulders and sleeves in such a way that the arms can be lifted.

When the owls are disclosed, a bright speaker introduces them as the very wise officials leading the society's work. It was but a fact of well-known history, he goes on to explain, that the exercise of so much wisdom should produce this result, a bit of not only natural history, but *very* natural history. Unlike the specimens in most museums, he adds, these will be observed to be very much alive. As his speech continues, explaining the wisdom of various lines of work done or attempted and the reasons why such work should be encouraged, the owls nod solemnly, occasionally varying the exercises by inquiring gravely: "To which? To whom?" (To whit! To who-o-o!) at appropriate pauses. The speaker must answer these questions. For instance, he presents an appeal for whatever is most needed — more workers for a certain project, more funds to carry it out, more students of a course of missionary reading — anything that it is desired to forward.

"Who will be the first to respond?" he asks after explaining the plan. "To which one of you will belong the honor of heading the list of recruits for this very much needed work?"

"To which? To who-o-o-m?" echo the owls.

The speaker follows this up by getting the signatures or agreements desired, after which the entertainment is brought to a speedy close with some remark to the effect that the owls themselves are now likely to be outdone by the new workers, that they may have to yield the palm to those of still greater achievements. Here the owls flap their wings excitedly and ask their usual question, "To which? To who-o-o-m?" which may, the speaker adds, be left for the new workers to determine.

The natural history could be varied if any one is willing to impersonate a donkey in a similar way, the donkey to represent those who always say "Nay" to every opportunity to learn about the methods and literature of the society's work. This sad result could be used as a terrible example and every one be urged to inform and equip himself without delay, lest a similar fate overtake him. This feature should be incidental, the owls being much more prominent. When the speaker's comments become too embarrassing for the quondam donkey, the latter can hide his diminished head by dodging behind the rear curtain, leaving the owls in full possession.

LIVING CHECKERS

This novel form of entertainment was given in a California church one evening with noteworthy success. The platform was marked off in squares like a checker-board. Twelve little boys dressed in black and twelve little girls in white were the checkers.

A game was played behind the scenes by the two best checker-players of the town, and every move they made was duplicated on the stage, the child walking off when jumped. The kings were crowned with gold paper crowns.

After the game the children all came on the stage and executed a pretty march.

One method of regulating the moves of the "living checkers" would be by means of numbers. That is, give each child a number and mark the checkers to correspond; then have some one stationed behind the scenes to watch the game and call off the directions to the children by number, as fast as each move is made.

EASTER LILY DRILL [1]

By Imogen A. Storey

For this are required a number of little girls of uniform height. The costumes should be made of white crêpe de chine, cotton crape, cheesecloth, or other soft white material; and with them should be worn white sandals and stockings. Butterfly wings may be added, constructed of wire, covered with gauze. Each child should be provided with two stalks of Easter lilies, artificial lilies being preferable.

The decorations for the stage should be white and green, the Easter lily being prominent among the flowers used. The floor should be laid off with chalk as shown in the diagrams, to prevent mistakes in marching and floor positions.

If the drill is to be given in a Sunday-school room, the children may enter from behind the Bible-stand, which should be a mass of lilies; if out-of-doors or in a schoolroom, they may enter from behind a clump of shrubbery or a screen covered with Easter lilies.

[1] By courtesy of the Designer Publishing Co.

The children enter on lines as shown in Diagram A, holding lilies in the outside hand extending up and slightly out at the side, with the elbow bent. When they reach the lines R and L on diagonal lines from the rear, they begin a fancy step executed as follows: Charge diagonally forward with the inside foot, holding the lilies extended high above the head, with the elbow straight and the hand even with the head; first count. Kneel on the outside knee and let the lilies fall forward till the tops touch the floor;

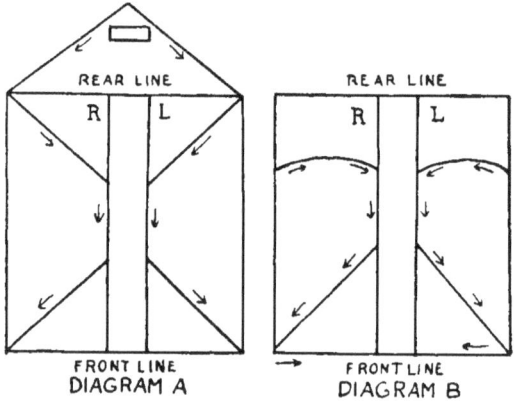

second count. Stand to charge position, holding the lilies as before; third count. Bring the heels together (drawing the foot in the rear to the forward one); fourth count. This finishes the first part of the step.

Charge diagonally forward with the outside foot, changing the lilies to the opposite hand; first count. Drop on the inside knee and bring the lilies to position, falling forward, touching the floor; second count. Stand to the charge position the same as before; third count. Heels together; fourth count. Continue this step to the front line.

EASTER LILY DRILL

On reaching the front line the march is resumed and they cross to the opposite side, as shown by arrows in Diagram B, those on the left marching in front of those on the right. They turn toward the rear and then turn on curved lines to the lines R and L, as shown in Diagram B.

When they reach the lines R and L they begin a fancy step executed as follows: Divide the lily stalks, holding one in each hand; extend both arms shoulder-high to the front and point diagonally forward with the inside foot, touching the toe to the floor; first count. Sway forward and swing both arms shoulder-high at the side, holding well back, and look up, with the rear toe touching the floor; second count. Back to the first position; third count. Place the forward foot straight forward flat on the floor and bring the heels together (bringing the rear heel up to the forward foot); fourth count.

Repeat the motion until the diagonal lines in B are reached; then change to the following: Extend the inside toe diagonally forward and touch it to the floor, with both knees perfectly straight, and swing the arms straight beside the head; first count. Bend the forward knee and extend the inside arm diagonally up at the side, with the outside hand on the chest; second count. Kneel and bring the arms into position with the lilies falling forward, touching the floor; third count. Repeat the second count for the fourth count. Repeat the first count for the fifth count. Bend the forward knee and bring the lily to position extending high above the head; sixth count. Repeat the first count for the seventh count. Place the forward foot straight forward; change the weight to it and bring the heels together; eighth count. Repeat to the opposite side and continue alternating until the front line is reached.

On reaching the front line they turn to the rear on the side lines and resume the march, holding the lilies as at the entrance. On reaching the centre of the rear they fall into single file and march down the centre line shown in Diagram C without changing the position of the lilies. On reaching the front line the leader turns to the right on the diagonal line which forms the front point of the star in Diagram C, and the next turns to the left in the same way. They all turn, alternating, and march on lines forming the star and halting in the rear at a signal on the cross lines; the others halt on the dots.

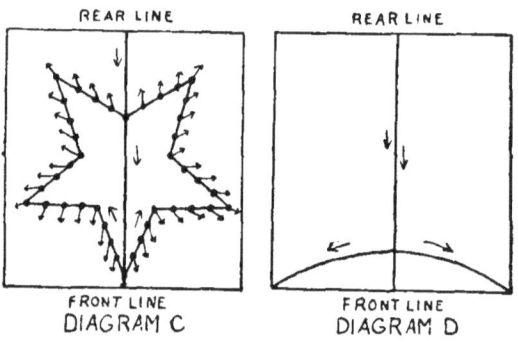

DIAGRAM C   DIAGRAM D

After halting a signal is given and they turn, facing in the same direction, and march around the star to the right. After they have circled the star once or twice a signal is given to halt; then another signal is given to turn facing in the direction shown by arrows in Diagram C. At the same time each child divides the lilies she holds, taking one stalk in each hand. All charge with the inside foot in the direction as shown by arrows in Diagram C and extend the inside arm diagonally up at the side, with the outside hand on the chest. Those on outside points of the star charge straight forward to the right, kneel on the left knee, and let the lilies fall forward, touching the floor. Those on inside points charge straight forward with the right foot and swing both arms straight forward and up beside the head, holding the lilies so that they meet overhead; first count. Those on outside points stand to charge position; second count. All bring their heels together, the front heel drawn back to the rear foot, and hold their arms down at the side; third count. All turn in the same direction; fourth count. Hold the lilies as at entrance. The march is resumed. After marching around the star to the left repeat the charging with counts, then repeat marching to right and left, holding the lilies as at the entrance, only a stalk in each hand.

After circling the star the last time they do not halt, but the girl on the front middle point marches to the front line and turns to the left. The next girl on the right follows and turns to the right. They all follow in the same way and march to the rear, fall into single file as before, and march down the centre as in Diagram D, turning on the curved lines. After forming on this line a signal is given to halt, another to turn, facing front. After they have turned facing front they may sing together an appropriate Easter song. After that they resume the march, turning to the rear on the side lines, and march out on the same lines as on entering, holding the lilies as at the entrance.

A SEVEN DAYS' WONDER

UNDER this bright title the Juniors of an Ohio society gave an entertainment in which the seven days of the week were represented. At the beginning a programme was rendered, consisting of recitations, short papers, and sacred songs. This represented Sunday.

For the other six days of the week there were booths. These were easily made by using one side of the Sunday-school room. In each of the booths articles were sold which were in accord with the day of the week which the booth represented. Monday's booth sold clothespins, starch, soap, washing-soda; Tuesday's, ironholders (made by the Junior girls), beeswax, and clothes-bags; Wednesday's, thimbles, needles, pins, pincushions, and sewing-bags; Thursday's, small brooms, dust-pans, dust-caps; Friday's, lemonade, peanuts, cake; Saturday's, chicken pie, pie, cookies, doughnuts.

The Juniors were very much interested, each one giving one or more articles for the booths.

The boys had entire charge of the Friday booth and took the offering during the rendering of the programme.

Such a programme might suitably include one or more of the following three recitations; an exercise, either "The Junior Medical School" or "The Creeds of the Bells," which are also included here, or "A Letter Exercise" for the smaller ones.

Lifting and Leaning

Recitation for a boy or girl

There are two kinds of people on earth to-day,
Just two kinds of people; no more, I say.

Not the good and the bad, for 'tis well understood
The good are half bad and the bad are half good.

Not the happy and sad, for the swift-flying years
Bring each man his laughter and each man his tears.

Not the rich and the poor, for to count a man's wealth
You must first know the state of his conscience and health.

Not the humble and proud, for in life's busy span
Who puts on vain airs is not counted a man.

No! the two kinds of people on earth I mean
Are the people who *lift* and the people who *lean*.

Wherever you go, you will find the world's masses
Are ever divided in just these two classes.

And strangely enough you will find, too, I ween,
There is only one lifter to twenty who lean.

In which class are you? Are you easing the load
Of overtaxed lifters who toil down the road?

Or are you a leaner who lets others bear
Your portion of worry and labor and care?
— Ella Wheeler Wilcox

If I were Japanese

Recitation to be given by a little girl in Japanese costume

If *I'd* been born across the seas,
In a little home of clean bamboo,
Among the flowering cherry-trees;
If *I'd* been fed on fish and rice,
And the queerest nuts that ever grew;
If *I'd* been used to a jinrikisha,
And never seen a railroad-car —
Perhaps it wouldn't seem so nice
    To be a Japanese.

But "Mary Jane" does seem so plain
Compared with "Neo Ina San,"
And such a place as "Jones's Creek"
(That's where I live and must remain)
Could not be found in all Japan!
Instead of "Pike's" and "Skinner's Peak,"
Of Fujiyama there they speak,
The sacred mountain by the seas.
How elegant geographies
    Must be in Japanese!

We have such very common things,
Like pigs in pens and coops of hens,
Round-corner stores that smell of cheese,
While they have storks with spreading wings,
That live among the reedy fens.
Their girls have paper parasols
And painted fans, as well as dolls.
They wade in flowers to their knees,
And live a life of joyous ease,
    The happy Japanese.

Yet mamma wouldn't be the same
With beady eyes and funny name,
And might not care so much for me,
And — come to think — they never can
Have any Christmas in Japan!
They worship curiosities,
Great metal idols made by man
About the time the world began.
So on the whole I'd rather be
A little plain American.
An imitation, if you please,
    Not truly Japanese.
               — Clara E. Dolliver

DREAMING AND DOING

Recitation for a little girl

Little Amy sits alone
  In a cool and bowery place,
With her book and bonnet thrown
  Down beside her, and her face
  Showing, 'mid its childhood's grace,
More than childhood's thoughtfulness:
What her thoughts are, can you guess?

She is thinking, "Were I grown
  Up to be a lady tall,
With a grand house all my own,
  Pictures hanging round the wall,
  Servants ready for my call,
Tell me, heart, and tell me true,
What should all my money do?"

Whether Amy e'er will grow
  Up to be that lady tall,
Know I not; but sooth I know,
  In a cottage low and small,
  Where no servants wait her call,
Doth a careworn mother's brow
Tell where help is needed now.

Not by dreams, but deeds of grace,
  Willing heart and hand are shown;
Smallest cot hath ample space
  For the love in helping known,
  Love that seeketh not her own.
Little Amys, if I knew them,
I would softly whisper to them,
"*Dream* not lovely things, but *do* them."
               — W. M. L. JAY

The Junior "Medical School"

The following Junior exercise is from *The Christian Endeavor News* of Australia. It is meant to be given by nine boys, one of whom acts as leader. The other eight each carry medicine-bottles.

LEADER. I am neither a doctor nor a druggist, but I have here several notable remedies for complaints from which many people suffer. With a view to relieving any case of suffering here this evening, my friends will introduce to your notice the various remedies. Be assured they are not quack mixtures, but every one of them tried and proved medicines, recommended by all who have used them.

1. For that tired feeling, especially good for ministers on Monday morning, for Sunday-school teachers and Christian Endeavorers, take a liberal dose of 2 Chron. 15: 7: "Be ye strong, therefore, and let not your hands be weak; for your work shall be rewarded."

2. This is especially good for housewives and all who work at home. When the kitchen chimney smokes and the butcher forgets to call, and things generally go wrong, try what a drink of Phil. 4: 4 will do for your feelings: "Rejoice in the Lord alway; and again I say, Rejoice."

Solo, "Be glad in the Lord, and rejoice."

3. This is a fine tonic for all who suffer from weak knees and shaky backbones. When you feel inclined to wabble and fall, instead of standing firm and walking straight, take a draught of Eph. 6: 10, 11: "Finally, my brethren, be strong in the Lord and in the power of His might. Put on the whole armor of God, that ye may be able to stand against the wiles of the devil."

4. For business folks, when they feel like worrying over money matters and the bad state of trade and the keenness of competition, kill the germ of worry by taking a full tablespoonful of Phil. 4: 6: "Be careful for nothing, but in everything by prayer

A SEVEN DAYS' WONDER

and supplication with thanksgiving let your requests be made known unto God."

5. Especially recommended for school boys and girls if lessons are hard, teachers are cross, and others seem to be getting on better than they are. See what a real big dose of Isa. 41:13 will do: "For I the Lord thy God will hold thy right hand, saying unto thee, Fear not; I will help thee."

6. For all married folks, and for all those who hope to marry, squabbles and differences will be settled and life made bright and pleasant by finding Amos 3:3 and marking the place for future use: "Can two walk together except they be agreed?"

7. For all who fail to keep sweet, especially crabbed and crotchety people. When inclined to be snappy with everybody and everything, take down from the shelf Prov. 16:32 and imbibe freely: "He that is slow to anger is better than the mighty, and he that ruleth his spirit than he that taketh a city."

8. This is very comforting for all old folks. When you feel old age creeping on, take a whole bottle of Isa. 46:4 and then get a fresh bottle for future use: "And even to your old age I am he, and even to hoar hairs will I carry you: I have made, and I will bear; even I will carry, and will deliver you."

LEADER. We do not intend to take any fee for our medical advice. We only want you to try and prove our remedies for yourself.

Hymn, "The great Physician now is near."

THE CREEDS OF THE BELLS

Eleven of the older Juniors or Intermediates may give this selection, a slight variation of George W. Bungay's poem, which should be rendered with marked clearness and expression. Each stanza is recited by a different speaker, except the final one, which is to be given by all in chorus. When that portion is reached, it would be effective if each speaker were to produce a Christian Endeavor banner previously concealed.

At rallies the parts descriptive of their own denominations may be given to children from the different churches represented as far as convenient.

1. How sweet the chime of the Sabbath bells!
   Each one its creed in music tells,
   In tones that float upon the air,
   As soft as song, as pure as prayer;
   And I will put in simple rhyme
   The language of the golden chime;
   My happy heart with rapture swells
   Responsive to the bells, sweet bells.

2. "In deeds of love excel! excel!"
   Chimed out from ivied towers a bell.
   "This is the church not built on sands,
   Emblem of one not built with hands;
   Its forms and sacred rites revere,
   Come worship here! come worship here!
   In rituals and faith excel!"
   Chimed out the Episcopalian bell.

3. "O heed the ancient landmarks well!"
   In solemn tones exclaimed a bell.
   "No progress made by mortal man
   Can change the just, eternal plan;
   With God there can be nothing new;
   Ignore the false, embrace the true,
   While all is well! is well! is well!"
   Pealed out the good old Dutch church bell.

4. "Ye purifying waters, swell!"
   In mellow tones rang out a bell.
   "Though faith alone in Christ can save,
   Man must be plunged beneath the wave,

A SEVEN DAYS' WONDER

    To show the world unfaltering faith
    In what the Sacred Scripture saith.
    O swell! ye rising waters, swell!"
    Pealed out the clear-toned Baptist bell.

5. "Not faith alone, but works as well,
    Must test the soul!" said a soft bell.
    "Come here and cast aside your load,
    And work your way along the road,
    With faith in God, and faith in man,
    And hope in Christ, where hope began;
    Do well! do well! do well! do well!"
    Rang out the Unitarian bell.

6. "Farewell! farewell! base world, farewell!"
    In touching tones exclaimed a bell.
    "Life is a boon to mortals given
    To fit the soul for bliss in heaven.
    Do not invoke the avenging rod;
    Come here and learn the way to God;
    Say to the world, 'Farewell! farewell!'"
    Pealed forth the Presbyterian bell.

7. "To all, the truth we tell! we tell!"
    Shouted in ecstasies a bell.
    "Come, all ye weary wanderers, see!
    Our Lord has made salvation free!
    Repent, believe, have faith; and then
    Be saved, and praise the Lord, Amen!
    Salvation's free, we tell! we tell!"
    Shouted the Methodistic bell.

8. "In after-life there is no hell!"
    In raptures rang a cheerful bell.
    "Look up to heaven this holy day,
    Where angels wait to lead the way;

There are no fires, no fiends to blight
The future life; be just and right.
No hell! no hell! no hell! no hell!"
Rang out the Universalist bell.

9. "The Pilgrim Fathers heeded well
My cheerful voice," pealed forth a bell.
"No fetters here to clog the soul,
No arbitrary creeds control
The free heart and progressive mind
That leave the dusty past behind;
Speed well, speed well, speed well, speed well!"
Pealed out the Independent bell.

10. "No pope, no pope to doom to hell!"
The Protestant rang out a bell.
"Great Luther left his fiery zeal
Within the hearts that truly feel
That loyalty to God will be
The fealty that makes men free.
No images where incense fell!"
Rang out old Martin Luther's bell.

11. "All hail, ye saints in heaven that dwell
Close by the cross!" exclaimed a bell.
"Lean o'er the battlements of bliss,
And deign to bless a world like this;
Let mortals kneel before this shrine,
Adore the water and the wine!
All hail, ye saints, the chorus swell!"
Chimed in the Roman Catholic bell.

All

Harmonious in the wondrous chime
From neighboring vale to distant clime,

A SEVEN DAYS' WONDER 115

A bell with sweet, familiar sound
Rings, "Let the Prince of peace be crowned;
Walk in the light, and ever search
For ways to serve our Christ and church.
A glorious union we foretell!"
Thus speaks the Christian Endeavor bell.

A Letter Exercise

This is for nine of the smaller children, each carrying or wearing a large letter printed on a square of cardboard. The letters could be shown one at a time as each finishes speaking; but the more effective way is for the letters to be kept concealed till the close of the recitation; then all are produced at once, as the words which they spell are pronounced by all.

1. There's a great but simple rule
    Worth more than tongue can tell;
   At work or play, at home or school,
    'Tis useful just as well.

2. It changes gloomy days to bright,
    And often eases pain,
   Makes snarls and tangles come out right
    And difficulties plain.

3. 'Twill drive away the crossest frown,
    Oft making friends of foes;

4. The weary task I've seen it crown
    With patience and repose.

5. It makes the face look smooth and fair
    Though plain the features be;

6. The hardest cross it helps us bear
    With sweet humility.

7. In rain or shine, in heat or cold,
'Tis just the rule to mind;

8. The rich or poor, the young or old,
Its helpfulness may find.

9. What is it? would you like to know?
With meaning 'tis replete.
Whate'er you do, where'er you go,
Why, simply this: KEEP SWEET.

HIGH JINKS ALONG THE MILKY WAY
A ROMANCE OF THE ZODIAC
BY REV. VINCENT VAN MARTER BEEDE

CHARACTERS

CASSIOPEIA, queen of the constellations.
ANDROMEDA, her daughter.
PERSEUS, a high and mighty athlete, owner of the auto-comet.
ORION, a hunter.
GAZAN PEAQ ABOU, an astronomer from Araby and now chauffeur to Perseus.
CENTAUR, a mounted policeman, guardian of the highway.
BOÖTES, the milk-wagoner.
AQUARIUS, a water-carrier, servant at the House of Fortune.

SCENE

[*An airy apartment in the House of Fortune, the palace of* QUEEN CASSIOPEIA. *The rear "walls" are of flowing, blue-black drapery spangled with silver stars. The main entrance at the centre, rear, is concealed. When the curtains are pushed aside, they disclose a full moon with winking eyes and a smiling mouth. In the*

HIGH JINKS ALONG THE MILKY WAY

upper spaces of the apartment are hung Japanese-lantern planets and cardboard silhouettes representing the Great Bear and Little Bear, the Crab, and other signs of the zodiac. At the left a table bearing a pair of scales and a bowl of fishes. Just to the right of the centre is a large chair with a lid seat which opens like a shirt-waist box. Farther to the right is an owl perched on a conventional stand. The eyes of the bird are luminous. CASSIOPEIA *is discovered seated in her chair, her chin resting on her hands*]

[*Enter* ANDROMEDA, *carrying a child's toy balloon*]

ANDROMEDA. What's the matter, mother dear? You seem sad and troubled. [*Puts her arms about the neck of* CASSIOPEIA]

CASSIOPEIA. Yes, my darling, I am under a cloud. I am concerned about your future. I don't know whether I would rather have you marry the big, beautiful, but rough Orion or the well-bred but reckless Perseus.

ANDROMEDA. O mother, please do not speak about them now! What do you suppose this thing can be? [*Holding up the balloon*] It looks like a baby planet, but of course it isn't. It floated right up against our front door.

CASSIOPEIA. O, I know what it is. I once saw a large one. Hercules fished for it and used it for a football. This one is a child's balloon, a toy of one of the earth children.

ANDROMEDA. And see, mother, here is a tag tied to the — the balloon, and the writing is as follows: "If this reaches any of you nice, kind star people, won't you please drop down a Skye terrier to Jimsy McClumpha, 45 Tomato Alley, New York City?"

CASSIOPEIA. Dear little soul! He shall have one to-night. [*A crash is heard outside the door*] Gracious, what's that?

ANDROMEDA [*unconcernedly looking out through the doorway*]. It's nothing but a fallen meteorite, mother. It is so white-hot that it will be just splendid to cook pancakes on.

CASSIOPEIA. Call Aquarius, will you, please?

ANDROMEDA [*calling outside*]. A-qua-rius!

AQUARIUS. Coming at once, princess! [*Enter* AQUARIUS *with a jar of water. He bows to the queen and to* ANDROMEDA] Water, your Majesty?

CASSIOPEIA. No, thank you. I do wish, Aquarius, that you were as careful about keeping the palace tidy as you are about drawing water. Please get the broom and sweep up the star-dust.

AQUARIUS. Immediately, your Majesty.

[*He takes the broom from the corner in the left, and sweeps vigorously in the centre. Music is heard outside*]

CASSIOPEIA. The music of the spheres! What a lovely air!

ANDROMEDA. Yes, to-night it is Neptune. What is the news, Aquarius?

AQUARIUS. O, Taurus, the Bull, got loose and butted into Mars's new red gate-lamp. And of course your Majesty has heard about —

[*Enter, out of breath and very angry,* BOÖTES, *the milk-dipper in his hand*]

BOÖTES. Pardon, your Majesty.

CASSIOPEIA. What is it?

BOÖTES. Your Majesty, this thing has got to stop! I won't stand it!

CASSIOPEIA. What ails you, my good milk-wagoner?

BOÖTES. Why it's that good-for-nothing, sporty Perseus and his Arabian chauffeur and his awful auto-comet!

[CASSIOPEIA *tries not to smile,* ANDROMEDA *laughs behind her handkerchief, and* AQUARIUS *chuckles out loud*]

CASSIOPEIA. What has Perseus done now?

BOÖTES. He was scorching along the highway as usual, and he didn't blow his ram's-horn until he was almost on top of me. My dragons began to rear, and the front part of that fiery, hissing machine struck one of my back wheels, and knocked over my wagon, and spilled me and all the milk, galaxies and galaxies and galaxies of it! I tell you, I saw stars!

HIGH JINKS ALONG THE MILKY WAY 119

AQUARIUS. And now the highway will be called the Milky Way, I suppose.

BOÖTES [*roaring*]. You be quiet, water-carrier!

AQUARIUS. Remember the day that you borrowed water from me to mix with your milk? And after this the spilled milk will be more sky-blue than ever!

CASSIOPEIA. Hush! Hush! Both of you!

[BOÖTES, *lifting his dipper, makes for* AQUARIUS, *who dodges, laughing, around* CASSIOPEIA'S *chair and finally makes his escape through the doorway, where he applies the soft end of the broom to* BOÖTES]

CASSIOPEIA. Boötes, come to order this instant!

BOÖTES [*dropping on his knees before the queen*]. Pardon, chief glory of the constellations!

CASSIOPEIA. Granted, but only because you have good cause to be annoyed. I am exceedingly troubled to learn that my Twins can have no milk for their supper. Poor darlings, what will they do?

BOÖTES. I am very sorry, your Majesty. I will milk the goats of Mars for your especial benefit, and at once, if you desire.

CASSIOPEIA. Thank you. Andromeda, where are the Twins?

ANDROMEDA. Cousin Antinonus has taken them to the merry-go-round on Saturn's outside ring.

CASSIOPEIA. Then they are perfectly safe. They do so enjoy the flying horses and the other animals of the starry Zoo. But about this disgraceful scorching by the auto-comet. Did Centaur, the mounted policeman, witness the collision?

BOÖTES. Yes, he must have heard the thunderclap very distinctly. He galloped up to the wreck, but he was five minutes late.

AQUARIUS [*poking his head through the curtain*]. Then Centaur has turned into a milk-white steed. I say, Boötes, please come out and make yourself useful by brushing a few cobwebs off the sky.

[*The head of* AQUARIUS *is withdrawn*]

BoÖTES [*furiously shaking his dipper in the direction of* AQUARIUS]. O, just let him wait a little while.

[*A terrific scraping noise is heard outside*]

CASSIOPEIA AND ANDROMEDA [*jumping and stopping their ears*]. O-o-o!

[BoÖTES *rushes to the doorway, and there collides with the water-carrier, who gives* BoÖTES *a great shove*]

ANDROMEDA [*coming between them*]. Peace! Peace! Silence! Aquarius, what was that dreadful noise?

AQUARIUS. Don't be alarmed, princess. It was nothing but one of those sky-scrapers coming through. The hole can easily be patched with raincloud cement.

[*Exit* AQUARIUS]

CASSIOPEIA. Boötes, I should like to see the wreck. How far away is it?

BoÖTES. Not more than sixty-eight million miles, your Majesty.

CASSIOPEIA. Is that all? Then I will go by all means. A-qua-rius!

AQUARIUS [*cautiously poking his head through the curtain*]. Yes, your Majesty!

CASSIOPEIA. I want immediately my chariot drawn by swans, geese, and cranes.

AQUARIUS. Your order shall be obeyed, your Majesty.

[*The head of* AQUARIUS *is withdrawn*]

CASSIOPEIA. I will leave you in charge of the House of Fortune, Andromeda dear. Farewell, I shall be gone only a few æons. [*Embraces her daughter*]

ANDROMEDA. Farewell, dearest mother!

[*Exeunt* CASSIOPEIA *and* BoÖTES. *Enter* ORION, *with a bow and arrows. Two dogs are at his heels*]

ORION [*bowing and kissing the hand of* ANDROMEDA]. White beam of the evening, I salute thee.

ANDROMEDA [*laughing*]. Dear me, Orion, how long did it take you to make up that beautiful sentence?

ORION [*sighing*]. So still you do not care for me? Well, I suppose that I might as well stick to my hunting. I killed two lions just now, and I got on the trail of a unicorn. But what do you care for a rough hunter and his ways?

ANDROMEDA. O, I like you well enough, Orion, but —

ORION. I know! It is the slim proprietor of the auto-comet that is to your fancy. Come, come, my faithful pair [*to his dogs*]. Farewell, heartless watcher of the skies!

ANDROMEDA. Farewell, peerless hunter of the night! [*Exit* ORION *followed by his hounds*] I wonder whether Perseus has escaped from that horrid mounted policeman, Centaur, with his club and his shooting stars. [*Distant sound of a puffing motor-car, which evidently is drawing near to the House of Fortune*] The auto-comet! The auto-comet!

[*The machine has stopped. Enter* PERSEUS]

PERSEUS. My stars, Andromeda! I'm in a nice mess! The carburetor is out of gear. I can't get up a single spark of lightning. It's a bad breakdown, and Centaur, fully armed, is hot on my trail. My poor chauffeur, Gazan Peaq Abou, will fall into his hands as it is. The noble Arabian won't desert the auto-comet. I mustn't be arrested! I don't want to be exiled to the burned-out Moon for the rest of my nights. Can't you hide me?

ANDROMEDA. O, what shall I do? Here! Crawl into mother's big chair. There are plenty of air-holes in it.

PERSEUS. I will! Unending thanks!

[*He stows himself away in the chair.* ANDROMEDA *closes down the lid, then innocently goes to feeding the owl and the fishes. Sound of a galloping horse heard outside. Enter hastily* CENTAUR, *bearing in one hand a club, in the other a horse-pistol*]

CENTAUR. Excuse me, Princess Andromeda, but I am obliged to search this house for the criminal Perseus, who has not only been scorching in his auto-comet but has upset the milk-wagon of Boötes!

ANDROMEDA [*calmly taking a seat in the big chair*]. How dare you propose to search the House of Fortune, the palace of Queen Cassiopeia?

CENTAUR [*poking the draperies with his club*]. Sorry, princess, but all the stars and planets have to obey laws, you know!

ANDROMEDA. Do you expect an auto-comet to keep in any special orbit, I should like to know?

CENTAUR. Well, I see no signs of a hiding-place, but I may be obliged to make another search later on. Good-by, princess.

[*Exit* CENTAUR *at the left*]

ANDROMEDA. Meddling old thing!

[*Enter* CASSIOPEIA, BOÖTES, *and* AQUARIUS]

CASSIOPEIA. It's a shame! At any rate, the bag of gold will cover the expenses of your broken wagon and spilled milk, Boötes. [CASSIOPEIA *takes her daughter's place in the chair*] Thank you, my darling.

BOÖTES [*looking relieved and feeling of the bag which he carries*]. Yes, your Majesty.

ANDROMEDA. How did you get the money?

BOÖTES. Why, you see, princess, Aquarius found the bag lying on the highway.

ANDROMEDA. You mean the Milky Way.

BOÖTES. I suppose so, princess. My name was marked on the bag, and Aquarius turned it right over to me.

ANDROMEDA. I'm glad that you have become friends. Go on.

BOÖTES. Perseus must have dropped the gold from his machine for my benefit. He's not such a bad sort, after all.

ANDROMEDA. Then aren't you going to prosecute Perseus?

BOÖTES. No, princess, I wouldn't think of it, now that he's made up to me so handsomely. Boys will be boys.

[*Enter* CENTAUR, *with his hand on the collar of* GAZAN PEAQ ABOU]

CENTAUR. Here, at any rate, is the guilty chauffeur, your Majesty.

CASSIOPEIA. Arabian, you and your master merit a severe punishment; but as Perseus has paid Boötes a generous sum, and Boötes does not care to prosecute Perseus, that youth, when he is found, will merely be subject to fine or imprisonment for scorching.

CENTAUR. Very good, your Majesty, but —

ANDROMEDA [*eagerly*]. What is the extent of the fine, good Centaur?

CENTAUR. Five hundred pieces of gold.

ANDROMEDA. Aquarius, bring me that amount, please, from my private coffer.

AQUARIUS. At once. [*Exit* AQUARIUS]

CASSIOPEIA. My daughter, what are you thinking of?

ANDROMEDA. Mother, I have set my heart on doing this.

[*Enter* AQUARIUS *with bags of gold, which he weighs on the scales and then hands to* CENTAUR]

CENTAUR. I — I really am surprised, princess. The amount is quite correct. But Perseus —

ANDROMEDA. Then Perseus is really free?

CENTAUR. Yes, but can you tell me —

ANDROMEDA. Mother, will you do me the extraordinary favor of leaving your chair for a moment?

CASSIOPEIA [*rising*]. Certainly, my dear, but how odd a request!

ANDROMEDA. How sweet of you! [*Claps her hands*] Perseus! Come forth. All is well.

[PERSEUS, *stepping out of the chair, bows to the queen and the princess*]

PERSEUS. I am most grateful, my queen, for your unconscious hospitality.

CASSIOPEIA. You are quite welcome, but what a turn you have given me! Who would ever have supposed —

PERSEUS. I know that it was rude of me, and I apologize. Really, though, there was no other place to hide — except in the fish-bowl. And is my faithful chauffeur liberated as well?

CASSIOPEIA. Certainly.

PERSEUS. I thank you. Gazan, you are a free man! [GAZAN *prostrates himself before the queen*]

GAZAN. How can I thank you enough, my queen?

PERSEUS. Can you forgive me, my queen, my glowing orb? [*Kneels before* CASSIOPEIA, *who pats him on the head*]

CASSIOPEIA. Yes, indeed; only don't do it again, my dear young man.

PERSEUS. By the Medusa's head, I am your Majesty's to command! Splendid beacon of the night, I have a boon to ask.

CASSIOPEIA. What is it, pray?

PERSEUS. That I may have the hand of your daughter, in order that we may dance merrily through space together forevermore.

[ANDROMEDA *takes her place beside* PERSEUS]

CASSIOPEIA. Oh, how can I spare my only daughter?

ANDROMEDA. Mother, Perseus and I have loved each other a long, long time.

CASSIOPEIA. Take her, then, fearless slayer of the foul Gorgon sister. Only promise me one thing.

ANDROMEDA AND PERSEUS. What is that?

CASSIOPEIA. That you won't go scorching in the auto-comet during your honeymoon.

ANDROMEDA AND PERSEUS. We promise.

CASSIOPEIA. Then receive my blessing.

[*She seats herself in her chair.* ANDROMEDA *and* PERSEUS *kneel before her and she places her hands on their heads.* GAZAN PEAQ ABOU *and* CENTAUR *shake hands at the left.* BOÖTES *and* AQUARIUS *shake hands at the right*]

THE BEGGAR PRINCE
A CHILDREN'S ENTERTAINMENT
BY IMOGEN A. STOREY

SCENE I

[*Dining-room in the* KING's *palace. Old* KING COLE *and his young daughter are at table, with the* QUEEN *and company. The table is arranged at the rear end of the stage as shown in Diagram A. This table is made with a large hole in the centre, and the cloth should hang to the floor. Attendants, waiters, and pages occupy the stage when the curtain rises. The* KING *is very happy, laughing and making merry*]

KING [*calling*]. What, ho, without there! Bring hither my pipe and bowl. And let my fiddlers three be sent for, with all haste.

CHORUS OF GUESTS AND OTHERS [*confidentially, to audience*]. Old King Cole is a merry old soul; a merry old soul is he. He calls for his pipe, and he calls for his bowl, and calls for his fiddlers three.

[*The pipe is brought in by twelve pages dressed to represent tobacco leaves and flowers. The costumes should be alike and the children all as near the same size as possible. They enter at the rear of the table as shown by Diagram A, marching to music by twos, carrying the pipe on a large waiter. At the same time twelve little girls, also dressed to represent tobacco leaves and flowers, enter from the opposite side, carrying the bowl of tobacco; this bowl, which should be of old English make, is also on a large waiter. The music and march continue. On reaching the lines R and L a signal is given for all to halt together. Another signal is given for them to turn facing the table, and another to kneel. Four attendants take the waiters from their extended hands and place them on the table before the* KING. *Another signal and all rise together. Another and all face the lines R and L. They resume marching, turning single file on lines R and L, the front row on each side turning on the oblique lines, single file. When the leaders on lines R and L reach the cross line, they cross as is shown by arrows, meeting those from the diagonal lines, turning by twos on double lines to the front line. When the leaders on each double line reach the front line they turn, forming single file on each*

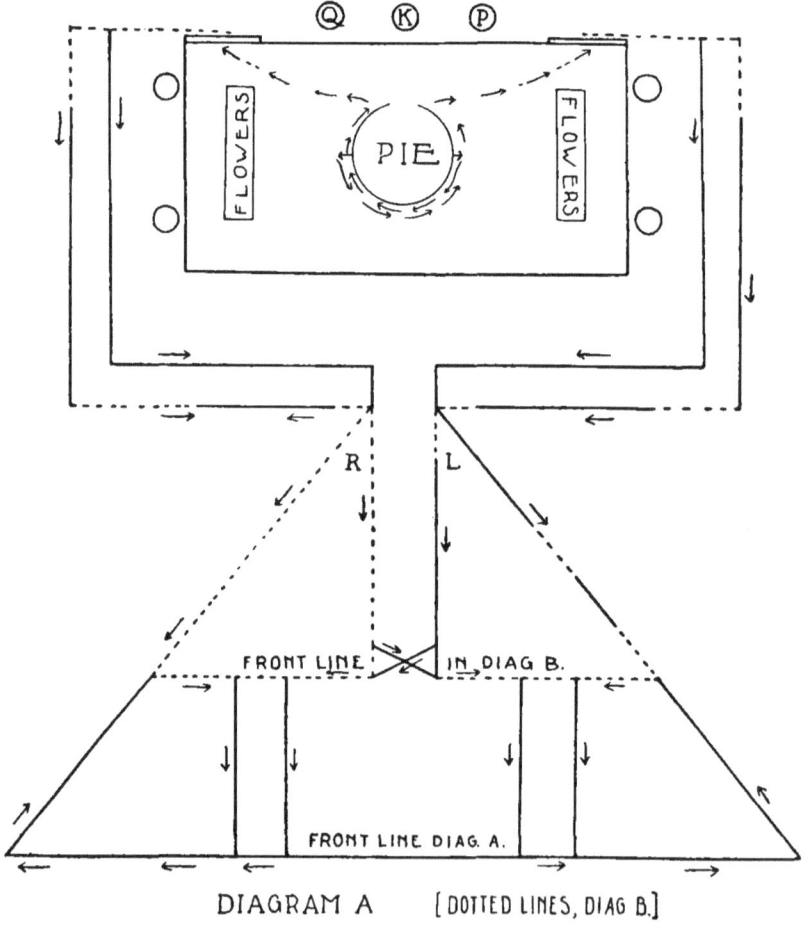

DIAGRAM A   [DOTTED LINES, DIAG B.]

THE BEGGAR PRINCE

side, and march out on oblique lines, turning by twos on reaching the double lines at the rear, and go out by twos]

KING. Now, ho, for my fiddlers three!

[*This part can be made as amusing as desired, and there will also be a chance to bring in special parts, such as reciting or singing. The* FOOL *of the court brings in the fiddlers, who should be vagabonds and their playing a burlesque. With them is a young lad with a mandolin. This boy should be selected for his voice. He should also be handsome in form and face and dressed in plain clothing. After the fiddlers have been heard, each in turn, the* FOOL, *who should be as witty as possible, gives a humorous recitation*]

KING. Truly, Fool, thou art truly a fool for want of sense. We will now hear the poor lad; and, if he can do nothing better than the rest, we will dismiss the whole of you as a sorry lot.

[*The lad sings. The young* PRINCESS *is attracted. When he has finished, she takes flowers from the table and throws to him. He picks them up and kisses them and bows and smiles to her. She forgets her father, stands up in her chair, and throws kisses with both hands to the young beggar* PRINCE. *The old* KING *in anger and surprise watches his daughter and the* PRINCE]

KING. Ah! what is all this wireless telegraphy? [*Looking from one to the other. He rushes from his seat at the table to the poor* PRINCE, *stamps his foot, and shakes his fist*]

KING. Begone, you vagabonds! [*Waving his hand in the direction of the fiddlers*] And you, my pretty beggar, with your yelping! How dare you thus insult my daughter, the future queen of No Man's Land? Begone, and never show your face again! Here is a sixpence for your song and a pocket of rye. Go till the soil, which is for such as you! [*Throws him a coin and a small bag*]

[*The* PRINCESS *throws herself into the arms of* FRIEDA, *a little Dutch maid who is her chum. Exeunt the poor* PRINCE, *the fiddlers, and* Fool. *The* King, Princess, Queen, *and company resume seats at the table. The* King *taps a bell on the table. Four attendants bring in an enormous pie and place it in the middle of the table. The pie is made of light wood or tin, with no bottom, and fits over the hole in the table. The table is arranged so that the children go up on steps into the pie and through on to the table, and until then are not seen by the audience. The top of the pie is made of paper. Two pages bring in a large knife]*

King [*rising*]. Four and twenty blackbirds baked in a pie. When the pie was opened, the birds began to sing. Now, wasn't that a dainty dish to set before a king? [*This can be either sung or recited*]

Attendants, Queen, Princess, Company [*in chorus*]. Indeed it was a dainty dish to set before a king.

King [*takes up knife and repeats*]. And when the pie was opened, the birds began to sing. Now, wasn't that a dainty dish to set before a king?

Others [*all together*]. Indeed it was a dainty dish to set before a king.

[*The* King *opens the pie. Four and twenty small children dressed to represent blackbirds come from the pie by twos as shown by Diagram B, circle around the table, all singing any selected song, and leave the table by slanting boards shown in Diagram B, and follow the lines as shown, turning to the front, running and flapping wings while singing. On reaching the lines R and L they turn on them and then on the front line. Turning on the diagonal lines, they run to the rear. Exeunt the same as the pages of the bowl and pipe. Curtain*]

Scene II

[*The stage should be changed to represent woods, a great many real flowers being introduced if this entertainment is given in summer. It would be very effective to give it in the woods. The beggar* Prince *is lying on a bank asleep, his instrument by his side.*

THE BEGGAR PRINCE

Enter FRIEDA, *dressed in the peasant's costume of Holland — wooden shoes, Dutch cap, short-waisted gown, etc. — followed by the* FOOL *of the* KING'S *court. They carry boughs of flowers*]

FRIEDA [*laughing*]. Oh, I have never yet seen such a funny man as you!

FOOL. Ah, but, my dear little Frieda, I am not always funny as you say. I am very sad when you do not listen to me. [*Sighs*] I sigh and moan [*sighs and moans*] and sigh when I am not trying to be funny, for my heart is breaking for you. [*Holds out his arms to her*]

FRIEDA. Tut, tut, yes, 'tis so, my lord. When you are not acting the fool, you are being a greater. [*Both laugh.* FRIEDA *sees the sleeping* PRINCE] Ho! ho! What is this? The bonny fellow who was at the palace yesterday. He looks sad, and it is not feigned as with you, but not so sad as my dear princess. 'Tis hard to wear a crown; but were I the princess and such a prince, though he be but a beggar, loved me, I would — well, I know what I would do.

FOOL. Well, now, let us hear what you would do. Treat him as you now do me, I trow?

FRIEDA. I would run away with him, and I would take his mandolin and go into the streets of London and sing with him; and we would live — O, it does not take much money for two who love.

[*She takes the mandolin and sings. The* FOOL *sings with her. (Note. These two should also be selected for their voices.) The* PRINCE *wakes. Sees* FRIEDA, *who is so fantastic with her flowers and wreaths*]

PRINCE. Is it a fairy queen indeed I behold at last? Ah, I was in hopes a real good fairy had come in my way. I dreamed that a fairy godmother had waved her wand and all my troubles had vanished. I have had so many misfortunes that I am sure she was absent at my birth. [*Bows his head on his hand*]

FRIEDA. O, cheer up, dear prince. I do not see why you should bemoan your fate. She loves you; and a woman, you know, will have her own way. And, mind you, it is only when the King has been too long smoking his pipe that he ceases to be merry and becomes cross. All may yet be well. I will take you to the Fairy Queen and intercede for you. This beautiful spot, you know, is Fairy Dell, and—ah, here is the queen of all the fairies now!

[*Music. The* FAIRY QUEEN *enters. A tall girl should be selected for this part. Her costume should be the handsomest of all the fairies'; it represents a rose of shaded pink. Her pages should be costumed in the same shades. In her hands she carries twenty-*

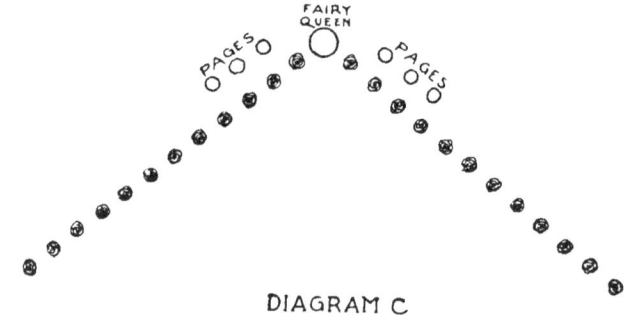

DIAGRAM C

four green garlands, two of a length, twelve to a hand. The other ends of the garlands should be carried by twenty-four small children dressed to represent rosebuds of the same color as the queen's dress. These children could be the same ones that represented the blackbirds in Scene I. The tiniest two should carry the longest garlands. The queen enters to music, driving buds, pages larger than the buds carrying her train. After driving around the stage she comes down the centre again and blows a whistle; all halt. Diagram C shows the position of halting. FRIEDA *runs to the queen*]

THE BEGGAR PRINCE

FRIEDA. O most noble Queen of the Fairies, in behalf of this poor prince I desire your attention.

[*Falls on her knee and kisses the queen's hand. The* PRINCE *steps up and also kneels and kisses her hand, then likewise the* FOOL]

FAIRY QUEEN. What wouldst thou have?

PRINCE. Most gracious Queen of the Fairies, I love the princess of this land; but her father, the King, despises me because, owing to my many misfortunes, I am now only a beggar prince. Look! He gave me a sixpence and this pocket of rye and bade me go till the ground and never show my face at the palace again!

FAIRY QUEEN. Thou hast done well to come to the fairies to have everything made right. Here, Swiftwing [*to one of her pages*], go you at once to the royal physician of the court and whisper this secret in his ear. Tell him the King is to take outdoor exercise and on no account to smoke any more. Be speedy! [*Exit* SWIFTWING, *running*] And now [*turning to the* PRINCE] hand me these gifts from our gracious and noble King of No Man's Land. [*Takes the bag and coin for a moment, then hands them back to him, speaking impressively*] Take the pocket of rye and make a wish, and every grain shall turn to one thousand pounds, and the pitiful sixpence shall represent six estates suitable for your bride, the Princess.

[*Enter* SWIFTWING. *The* PRINCE *now slips behind the scene and quickly changes his costume*]

SWIFTWING [*bowing to the queen*]. My errand is done already, fair Queen.

FAIRY QUEEN. 'Tis well. And now come one and all; we will go with the young lover to the palace and see whether he does not win the King's daughter. But he must not appear thus clad. I will first change our beggar into a true prince.

[*She waves her wand over the* PRINCE *as he re-enters and steps out from the crowd. The wand should be a lily branch. In rushes* the PRINCESS *from the opposite side. At first she sees only* FRIEDA, *who is standing a little apart from the rest*]

PRINCESS. At last I have found my Frieda. [*Throws her arms around* FRIEDA'S *neck*] I have looked for you everywhere. I was lonely, as I often am now. [*Sighs*] I wonder where the beautiful, poor prince is now.

PRINCE [*approaching her*]. Here he is, my beautiful Princess! [*Falls on his knee and kisses her hands*]

PRINCESS [*laughing and holding the* PRINCE'S *hand as he rises*]. The King was in the counting-house, counting out his money; the Queen was in the parlor, eating bread and honey; and so I thought I would run away and see if I could find my Frieda.

PRINCE. And so you found us both.

FOOL [*taking* FRIEDA *by the hand*]. The maid was in the garden, hanging out the clothes, when 'long came a blackbird, and nipped off her nose.

[*Here he pulls* FRIEDA'S *nose. All together repeat or sing*]

> Sing a song of sixpence,
>   A pocket full of rye,
> Four and twenty blackbirds
>   Baked in a pie.
> When the pie was opened,
>   The birds began to sing.
> Now, wasn't that a dainty dish
>   To set before a king?
>
> The King was in his counting-house,
>   Counting out his money;
> The Queen was in the parlor,
>   Eating bread and honey;
> The maid was in the garden,
>   Hanging out the clothes,
> Along came a blackbird,
>   And nipped off her nose.

[*The* FOOL *pulls* FRIEDA'S *nose, the* PRINCE *the* PRINCESS'S. *All repeat or sing*]

> Old King Cole is a merry old soul;
> A merry old soul is he.
> He calls for his pipe, and calls for his bowl,
> And calls for his fiddlers three.

[*Enter, hurriedly, the* KING *with two money-bags, the* QUEEN *with a slice of bread and honey, and two attendants*]

KING [*laughing heartily*]. Ha! ha! Not so, good friends. I have sent away my pipe and my bowl of tobacco, for I find smoking a bad habit. Yes, it is quite true. And, really, I don't mind; for I do feel better already for my brisk walk in the woods. Ha! ha! ha! So you thought you had given me the slip? [*Shakes his finger at the* PRINCESS. *Sees the* FAIRY QUEEN] But stay! Is this the domain of the Fairy Queen? [*Looking around*] Gracious madam, we mortals are intruding.

FAIRY QUEEN. Indeed, I bid you welcome.

KING [*turning to the* PRINCE]. And who is this distinguished stranger?

FAIRY QUEEN. That, O King, is the great Prince of the Six Kingdoms of Rye, now on his way to sue for the hand of your daughter.

[*The* PRINCE *approaches, with the* PRINCESS, *and both kneel before the* KING *and* QUEEN]

KING. Take her, and the half of my kingdom with her. [*Hands the* PRINCE *one of the two money-bags*] Truly, thou art a son-in-law greatly to my liking. What, ho, my fiddlers three! Come hither and let us be merry.

[*The* PRINCE *and* PRINCESS *rise and the* QUEEN *offers them bread and honey. Enter the fiddlers. All present repeat or sing*]

Old King Cole is a merry old soul,
  But merrier far is he
Since he said good-by to his pipe and his bowl,
  And called for his fiddlers three.

[*Music, in which the fiddles can occasionally be heard. Tableau or final march of all the characters*]

A WINDOW EVENING

WINDOWS are meant to give an outlook. They also let in light. Before this evening is at an end some new light and a broader outlook may be obtained regarding one of the live topics of the day, which will appeal strongly to all true Endeavorers of whatever age.

The evening as a whole can be made thoroughly entertaining, and the earlier part of the programme may introduce one or two humorous or semi-humorous features and several musical numbers. There might be a reading from Barrie's "A Window in Thrums," preferably the chapter on "Preparing to Receive Company." The music may include one or more songs which mention a window, such as "I Wonder," "Appear, Love, at thy Window," or "The Swallows" (words by Clifton Bingham, music by Frederic H. Cowen). Try to arrange for several instrumental selections to be rendered by a musician who is blind. There are so many blind people who play well that it will often be found possible to enlist one. This music will lead up to the next feature of the evening, "New Light on a Dark Subject."

A WINDOW EVENING

This should be a study of the needs of the blind and of the most practical methods of helping them. Do not be satisfied with merely arousing sentiment, nor with the superficial view which regards all blind persons as objects of charity, but study the situation carefully in advance, getting the latest facts obtainable from experienced workers among the blind. Find out what has been and is being done, what is *not* being done that should be, and just how Endeavorers can be to some extent genuine light-bearers to those that thus sit in darkness.

Much of interest can be learned from the books, "Dr. William Moon and his Work for the Blind," by John Rutherford, M.A., B.D., and Dr. Juval's "On Becoming Blind," as well as from the many sketches that have been published of Helen Keller and other eminent blind persons, including our own well-beloved Fanny Crosby, the writer of so many hymns prized by Christian Endeavorers. Perhaps the information with most of practical bearing on the subject to-day can be obtained from the magazine called *The Outlook for the Blind*, published at Cambridge, Mass. Articles by Dr. Samuel G. Howe, John B. Curtis, Helen Keller, and others who speak from knowledge abound in this magazine. Those on "Summer Schools for Blind Men," by Superintendent James J. Dow; "Historical Sketch of the American Association of Workers for the Blind," by Edward J. Nolan, the eminent blind Chicago lawyer, and "The Pennsylvania Home Teaching Society," by Dr. Robert C. Moon, giving a good idea of the work of his illustrious father, all in the issue for April, 1907, are especially noteworthy. Full information regarding the work for the adult blind, which is by far the largest and most generally neglected field, can be obtained by writing to Mr. Charles

E. Comstock, Superintendent of the Illinois Department of Visitation and Instruction of the Adult Blind, 5456 Lexington Avenue, Chicago.

With these helps two or more papers may be prepared; the blind musician, if a speaker, will of course be asked to contribute his own thoughts on the subject, and after consideration of "Some Things we Can do About it" the evening may close with more music. "Lead, Kindly Light," some of Fanny Crosby's hymns, or "Blind Bartimæus" would be good selections to use at this stage.

It would be interesting to have on view one or more of the books with raised letters, also a Braille writer, a shorthand-machine of the sort used by the blind, and the curious little grooved frame called a "slate" and the stylus with which they write, which could be examined by the audience at the close of the programme. Specimens of the work of the blind may be added.

SCENES FROM AMERICAN HISTORY

DIVIDED into three main groups — Colonial, Revolutionary, and Civil War times — our country's history furnishes many striking pictures which it is not difficult to present in tableau form. All three of the periods mentioned could be drawn upon for the same evening's entertainment, or each of them could form an entertainment in itself.

For Thanksgiving time a Colonial evening might suitably include a few scenes from the lives of the early New World explorers, Columbus and others. Very well known are the illustrations of "Columbus before the Council"

SCENES FROM AMERICAN HISTORY

and "Discovering America," also "Landing of the Pilgrim Fathers." Longfellow's "Evangeline" or "The Courtship of Miles Standish" will suggest a number of pleasing scenes.

One dark shadow in our early history, the Salem witchcraft superstition, is brought out impressively by Whittier's poem "The Witch's Daughter," which may be read, illustrated with one or more scenes. Or, without the reading, there may be two finely contrasted tableaux, "The Spinning Lesson" and "On Trial for Witchcraft," in both of which the same two characters, an old woman and her little granddaughter, may appear. Another effective contrast would be these: "A Colonial Tea Party, No. 1," showing three or four dainty little ladies in Colonial dress of different colors seated around a tea-table, one of them in the act of pouring the tea, and "A Colonial Tea Party, No. 2," showing men of stern visage busied in throwing the fated tea-chests into Boston harbor. (These two could appropriately be included in either the Colonial or the Revolutionary programme.)

A Colonial evening would not be complete without a few scenes with the Indians. One or more of these might well be from the life of John Eliot, the missionary who did so much for the red men. A paper or address telling of his work would be in order, with some glimpses of more recent developments in the work for the same race. The Indian Drill for little boys, described elsewhere in this book, may be introduced. Or have a Puritan Drill, which should be a rather sedate little march by a number of small girls dressed alike in Puritan costume, and close the evening by singing "America" or the "Thanksgiving Hymn."

In arranging the tableau "The Spinning Lesson" it is well to have not only the spinning-wheel with the little girl and the grandmother, but also a mother, who is watching the process smilingly, seated with one hand on the baby's cradle. During this tableau the music of "The Spinning-Wheel Cradle-Song" by Carolyn D. Merton would be especially effective.

For Washington's Birthday a similar programme may be based upon Revolutionary stories and poems. The famous cherry-tree tale may be the subject of the opening scene, giving the interview between the elder Washington and his son, the immortal George, who should be represented by the tiniest boy possible, dressed in exact reproduction of the George Washington costume, with an absurdly small toy hatchet. A little tree bearing red velvet cherries and with several gashes cut in its trunk or stem will make the scene more realistic. Then for the more serious scenes have the familiar boat picture of "Washington Crossing the Delaware"; a winter night scene showing the privations suffered in the camp at Valley Forge; the "Surrender of Cornwallis," which may include an effective march; "Washington at Trenton," with a troop of girls singing a song of welcome as they strew flowers at the feet of the advancing hero; and a group of the Washington family. These, together with a scene representing the celebrated statue of the Minuteman and a very pretty tableau of the "Daughters of Liberty," are all vividly described in detail in Miss Alcott's book "Jack and Jill," which can be found in almost any public library. Patriotic music is of course an essential feature of the evening, and one society on a similar occasion had a duet sung in costume by two "minutemen," entitled "We Are Two Men of a Bygone Age."

For Lincoln's Birthday decorate the platform with American flags and bunting, draped with immortelles. Prominently displayed should be a portrait of Abraham Lincoln and below it the words which he made immortal:

> With malice toward none;
> With charity for all.

The missions of the South may very appropriately be presented as a subject for attention.

Have a short address on the progress and needs of the freed people, and make the occasion one of helpfulness to their cause. If possible to secure it, one prominent feature of the evening might be a temperance address by some speaker who can give personal recollections of Lincoln; those by Major J. B. Merwin, for example, are enjoyed by young and old alike and are welcomed in churches everywhere.

The music should consist largely of the national songs interspersed with Southern ballads and one or two of the best negro melodies.

When, instead of speeches from outside, a more varied programme by the young people is desired, the following would be good, containing several novel features:

1. Music.
2. Recitation, "Abraham Lincoln."
3. Recitation, "O Captain! My Captain!"
4. Music.
5. Recitation by a boy, "Bay Billy."
6. Lincoln's Gettysburg Address.
7. Lincoln's favorite poem, "O, Why Should the Spirit of Mortal be Proud?"
8. Song, "Mighty Lak a Rose," or some other negro lullaby or plantation song.
9. Recitation, "The Pilot's Story."
10. Illustrated poem, Whittier's "Barbara Frietchie."
11. A Musical Allegory.
12. Flag Drill by children, closing with a tableau and singing of "The Star-Spangled Banner."

The poems can generally be found on inquiry at the public library. "Abraham Lincoln," by Richard Henry Stoddard, is in "Golden Numbers," a book of verse compiled by Kate Douglas Wiggin and Nora Archibald Smith and published by McClure, Phillips, and Company, New York. "Bay Billy," by Frank H. Gassoway, is in a volume called "My Recitations," compiled by Cora Urquhart Potter. Lincoln's Gettysburg Address and "The Pilot's Story," by William Dean Howells, are to be found in so many collections that there will be little trouble in getting hold of them. The same, of course, is true of Lincoln's favorite poem and Whittier's "Barbara Frietchie." The lullaby "Mighty Lak a Rose" is published by the John Church Company. It might be illustrated by a tableau of the faithful old colored "mammy" rocking her mistress's baby to sleep.

The "musical allegory" is one devised by Carolyn Wells and is given as follows: While the pianist plays "Columbia, the Gem of the Ocean," the curtain slowly rises, disclosing on a central raised platform a seated figure of Columbia, holding a large oval portrait of Abraham Lincoln framed in gold. Columbia should be a fair young girl with long golden hair, dressed in a costume like that of the goddess of Liberty.

Let the music now change to "Way Down upon the Suwanee River" as a figure representing Slavery glides slowly in from the left and kneels with supplicating gesture before the portrait, but slightly to the left.

Choose for this symbolic representation of Slavery a sweet, sad-faced girl, and dress her simply in a long, flowing robe of gray or brown, with her hands shackled by chains that clank as she raises her hands in entreaty. While Slavery still kneels, a figure of War enters at the right.

This must be a tall girl of commanding presence, strong features, and black hair and eyes. She is clad in black, or very dark steel-gray, carries a sword or a musket, and wears a helmet. She advances with firm, martial tread, while the pianist plays "The Battle-Hymn of the Republic." War takes her position, standing at the right of Columbia, and after this Peace enters at the rear. Peace is robed in pure white, with wings and a gilt crown. A dove rests on her shoulder and she carries an olive-branch. She mounts a pedestal behind Columbia and spreads her arms above the group in protecting fashion, while the music changes to "America." With carefully selected characters this whole scene can be made most beautiful and effective.

As for "Barbara Frietchie," the poem is to be read or recited and illustrated as follows:

Let a small company of boys dressed in the nearest convenient approach to the Confederate uniform march across the platform. When the leader is nearly opposite a window arranged in the rear of the platform, toward one end, Barbara Frietchie appears at the window. This should be one of the older girls, dressed in a simple dark dress, with whitened hair. She leans out of the window, waving the flag in defiance of the enemy.

A SURPRISE FLOWER GARDEN

COLLECT all the interesting little flower poems you can find which would make bright recitations or songs for children. Of these select such as refer to the especial kinds of flowers which can be most easily made out of paper — the blossoms, stems, and leaves. The blossoms must be cut very large, like sunflowers; you will have to improve on

A SURPRISE FLOWER GARDEN

nature considerably in the matter of size. The yellow centre of each blossom (brown in the case of the sunflowers) should be at least six inches in diameter.

Have a large curtain of brown for a background on which to arrange your floral surprise. Fasten the flowers on these, grouped at different heights, as you find prettiest and most convenient. When they are all securely in place, cut almost around the centre of each, through background and all, making of the yellow centre a little circular door that can be opened from behind. If necessary, these little doors can be lined with cardboard to make them more manageable. Label each one on the back with the name of its flower and a number, and fasten it in place when closed with a loop and button or similar device that can be quickly loosened.

The children should be carefully drilled to take their places behind the curtain without crowding or confusion, each one at the particular little door bearing his or her number. By having some of the children seated and others standing on boxes or steps all the desired variation of height can be secured.

Jack-in-the-Pulpit is to be master of ceremonies. Jack should be a bright but rather small boy dressed to look like a sprite, in close-fitting white or pale green, with little gauze wings made on a wire frame. The pulpit should represent the flower Jack-in-the-Pulpit and should be made of white and green tissue-paper over a frame of wire or light wood. This should be placed at the rear of the platform, in front of the "garden" background, though care should be taken that it does not conceal any of the flowers Jack is to introduce. He carries a small whistle concealed in a trumpetflower.

At the first view nothing is seen by the audience but the flower-decked curtain and the green and white pulpit standing near. Jack is stooping down in the flower, out of sight, until the signal is given for his appearance. The Junior superintendent or other person in charge now greets the audience as follows:

Friends, it gives me great pleasure to welcome you to my garden. When you have seen all its wonders, you will agree with me that it is quite the most remarkable flower garden in this part of the world. You have doubtless heard of the great size attained by the vegetation in southern California. These flowers that you see here are also fine, large specimens because — but I will leave it to my friend Jack-in-the-Pulpit to explain the reason. [*Calling*] Jack! O Jack! Are you asleep? Wake up and help me to introduce the other flowers to our friends who have come to see them.

JACK [*standing up in the flower and blowing a tremendous blast on his whistle*]. Does that sound as if I were asleep?

SUPT. [*with hands over ears*]. Dear me, no! I might have known you were wide-awake and only waiting to be called. But see here, Jack, all these good people have come to visit my garden. Will you help me to show it?

JACK [*bowing first to the superintendent and then to the audience*]. Indeed I will, with pleasure.

SUPT. Then I will leave you now in full charge for a little while. [*Exit, while* JACK *takes out his pointer made of a long green stalk or gigantic grass-blade and proceeds with his explanation, using his pointer freely as occasion suggests*]

JACK. You have noticed, good people, how large the flowers are which you see here. It is because they have been grown in the sunshine of Christian Endeavor, in which climate flowers of this kind flourish surprisingly well. Then, too, they grow by exercise; they are well rooted; they have abundance of fresh air

A SURPRISE FLOWER GARDEN   145

and are watered by showers of kindness. You see here the result of careful cultivation. I might preach a long sermon on this subject, but I will let this short one do for to-night. Now I will introduce the flowers and let each one speak for itself. [*Calling*] Snowdrop! [*Blows whistle*] Wake up, Snowdrop, and give an account of yourself!

Any other desired flower may be called first. As each flower is called, its little door is opened from the rear and the child puts his or her face to the opening and sings or recites, after which the face is withdrawn and the little door is closed again. Jack thus calls on one after another till all have responded. Then at a signal the little doors are all opened at once and the flowers, Jack and all, join in singing, as a climax, the song "Let a Little Sunshine In."

For the responses of some of the flowers the following are suggested. Where no introductory remark by Jack is indicated, he merely blows his whistle and calls the flower by name.

Crocus, Mayflower, Violet, Rosebud. Introduce this group with the preliminary remark by Jack, "Well, if here isn't one flower coming now without even waiting to be called! and she always brings some friends with her, too. [*Crocus appears, smiling.*] Hello! How did you happen to wake up so early?" Then the four recitations should follow in the words given in "The Waking of the Spring Flowers," to be found elsewhere in this book.

Apple Blossom. This one could recite "When the Apple Blossoms Stir," a delightful little poem by Lucy E. Tilley, once published in *St. Nicholas* and very likely in book form since.

Daffodils. For these have as many Juniors as possible, but they need not sing or speak. Let Jack recite the first stanza of Wordsworth's "I Wandered Lonely as a Cloud," and the daffodils respond merely by a smiling look through their little doors all together.

The Buttercup.

> Down in the fields one day in June
>   The flowers all bloomed together,
> Save one who tried to hide herself,
>   And drooped, that pleasant weather.
>
> A robin, who had flown too high,
>   And felt a little lazy,
> Was resting near this buttercup,
>   Who wished she were a daisy.
>
> For daisies grow so big and tall!
>   She always had a passion
> For wearing frills about her neck
>   In just the daisies' fashion.
>
> "Dear Robin," said this sad young flower,
>   "Perhaps you'd not mind trying
> To find a nice white frill for me
>   Some day when you are flying."
>
> "You silly thing!" the robin said,
>   "I think you must be crazy!
> *I'd* rather be my honest self
>   Than any made-up daisy.
>
> "You're nicer in your own bright gown;
>   The little children love you;
> Be the best buttercup you can,
>   And think no flower above you.

A SURPRISE FLOWER GARDEN

"Look bravely up into the sky,
And be content with knowing
That God wished for a buttercup
Just here where you are growing."

Bluebell. Use the "fairy-telephone" stanza of the Leaflet Motion Song given elsewhere in this book. Let Jack sing or recite the main part of the stanza at the tinkling of a silvery bell; then the little door should open and the bluebell child should respond with the refrain of that stanza.

Sweet Pea. One of the smallest girls should take this part. She may recite:

My name is really Polly,
Little Polly Lee;
But sometimes for a joke, you know,
They call me just "Sweet P."

Dandelion. Use the first part of the recitation in the Dandelion Drill. Let Jack give the opening lines through the words, "A-tripping o'er the meadow he is seen." The dandelion responds from where Jack leaves off, through the words "woodlark and the toad," only speaking in the first instead of the third person. Jack then gives the next four lines, ending, "All the children love him well."

Daisies. A group of three "daisies" may sing this song, each taking one stanza and all three joining in the chorus:

1. Out in the meadow so fresh and so dewy,
   Out in the fields at the breaking of day,
   Op'ning their eyes at the first beam of sunlight,
   "We wish you good-morrow," the daisies say.

Cho. Golden and white
In the morning light,
"We wish you good-morrow,"
The daisies say.

2. Out in the fields in the glory of noontide,
    Out where the bees and the butterflies play,
  With their bright eyes looking up into heaven,
    "We love the bright sunshine," the daisies say.
    Cho. Golden and white
    In the noontide light,
    "We love the bright sunshine,"
    The daisies say.

3. Out in the fields in the quiet, sweet starlight,
    Hushed all confusion and noise of the day,
  All fast asleep, with their golden eyes hidden,
    "We wake on the morrow," the daisies say.
    Cho. Golden and white
    In the still starlight
    "We wake on the morrow,"
    The daisies say.

The melody of the daisies' song runs as follows:

Pansy. There are many suitable poems on lovely thoughts, pansies, or heartsease; or use this quotation:

"If instead of a gem, or even a flower, we could cast the gift of a rich thought into the heart of a friend, we should be giving as the angels give."

Water-Lilies. If there are three of the Intermediates who are equal to easy part-singing, they might give Franz Abt's trio "The Water-Lily," to be found among Schirmer's first series of "Octavo Choruses for Women's Voices." If more of a similar nature are wanted, there are twelve flower poems by Edward Oxenford set to music in "Buds and Blossoms," Augener and Company's Edition of Vocal Duets, No. 8961d. But most of the flowers should be represented by Juniors.

Poinsettia. Let Jack introduce this blossom by saying: "There is one flower that in far-away lands used to bring thoughts of Easter; but in our own time and land it is at Christmas, merry Christmas, that we see it decking all the holiday gifts. The poinsettia brings us a message of Christmas cheer and good will."

Any little Christmas song or recitation may be the flower's response.

Easter Lily.

Easter at the Door

Known by many a sweet foretoken,
Many an age-long pledge unbroken;
By the silver slant of showers,
Peeping up from friendly flowers;
By the river all aquiver with the little rippling waves,
By the sod that groweth greener on God's acre, thick
    with graves;

Known by many a sign and token,
Many a thrill of life unspoken,
Lo! we greet love's purest angel!
Here is Easter at the door.

Star of Bethlehem. The first stanza or two of the poem "O Little Town of Bethlehem."

Very small flowers, even including forget-me-nots and lilies-of-the-valley, can be represented in clusters with the face looking through the midst of the cluster instead of from the centre of a single flower.

It will often be found a good plan to make this occasion one to secure all the practical encouragement possible from those present for any special "fresh-air" or flower-gardening project of the Juniors. Few will fail to respond to an appeal made by the superintendent or other friend of this phase of the Juniors' work. Let this come just before the final song by all the flowers, "Let a Little Sunshine In."

AN EVENING WITH THE GYPSIES

MANY who know something of the striking evangelistic work of "Gypsy" Smith will find it of interest to give a little thought to the roving, picturesque people from among whom he came. Besides being an attractive entertainment, this can easily be made an occasion for a brief study of gypsy life and its characteristics and possibilities in connection with home or foreign missions.

Arrange the platform to look like a gypsy camp in the woods. Have a tent concealing a door in the rear, through

AN EVENING WITH THE GYPSIES

which the musicians are to enter, and a large pot hanging on a tripod near by over a fire, which may be simulated by bright red paper tucked in and around small logs and sticks. An old gypsy woman may be in charge, occasionally poking the fire and stirring the contents of the pot. She may make a short speech of welcome to the audience, in which she announces the various parts of the entertainment except the drill, and at the close tell fortunes if versed in palmistry.

Some one should give a short sketch of "Gypsy" Smith's life and work, with a few interesting anecdotes in connection with it.

In the same or another address or paper bring out some of the chief characteristics of gypsy nature, with a brief account of the probable origin, history, laws, and customs of this nomadic people.

These features should be interspersed with music, such songs as "The Spanish Gypsy," "Esmeralda," or "Fiddle and I" as solos, or "The Woods, the Woods," an easy and pretty duet by Franz Abt for first and second soprano, to be found in "Twelve Two-Part Songs," Augener and Company's Edition, No. 8961a. Guitar, mandolin, or banjo solos would be in order, or combinations of these and other stringed instruments. Let all the musicians be dressed in gypsy costume and emerge from the tent.

Introduce as a surprise feature, without previous announcement, this gypsy drill, devised by Imogen A. Storey:

An even number of children dressed in bright gypsy costumes should run in from behind bushes (or screens made of branches and flowers placed on each side of the tent) and follow the lines as shown in A, beating their tambourines, which should be tied with bright ribbons to match the costumes. They follow the lines in A, running to music and beating their tambourines, turn on the front line and then to the rear again as shown by the arrows, then on the diagonal lines. When the leaders reach R and L, the old woman should give the command, "Company, halt!" All should halt at the same time, keeping the regulation distance from the one in front, about twenty inches. In order to do this the command should be given while either foot is in advance, then bring the rear foot up beside the one in advance, letting the heels sink at the same time and bringing the arms

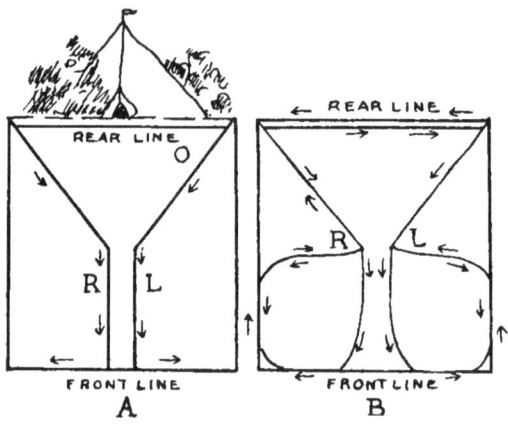

down at the side. Now let there be a few words of explanation and announcement from the old woman. She then gives the command, "Forward, march!" Here the music should begin again and the children do this fancy step with arm movements. Swing the inside arm curved over the head, holding the tambourine in the inside hand, and advance the inside foot (keeping the knee straight) diagonally forward to the inside and touch the toe to the floor, first count; swing the inside arm out at the side and down and hit the tambourine with the outside hand, second count; grasp the tambourine in the outside hand and swing the outside arm curved over the head, and advance the

AN EVENING WITH THE GYPSIES 153

outside foot (after placing the inside foot flat on the floor and changing the weight to it) and touch the toe to the floor, third count; swing the outside arm out at the side and down and hit the tambourine with the inside hand, fourth count. Continue this, advancing and following the lines in B as shown by arrows. When the leaders reach the lines R and L in going to the rear the command is given, "Direct step, march!" and the music should change to a common march. The march should be begun by all at the same time, the same as in halting, and all should place their hands on their hips. On reaching the rear they cross to the opposite side as shown by arrows and come down the diagonal lines again with a "swing-cross step," with hands still on the hips.

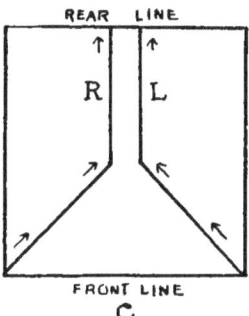

C

Advance the inside foot diagonally inside and place it on the floor, first count; change the weight to it and swing the outside leg in front of it, keeping the knee straight and the toe turned out, second count; swing the outside leg back to the outside and place the foot on the floor diagonally forward to the outside, third count; change the weight to the outside foot and swing the inside leg across in front of the outside, fourth count. Continue this step, which should be rather quick, and come down lines R and L in B. On reaching the ends of the front line the "skip step" familiar to all children should be begun. They skip on the lines shown in C and go out by twos. They soon appear again from the tent with small tin plates of cake and tissue-paper napkins, also little fancy tin cups, which the old woman fills from the pot. This may be an ice or lemonade. The children now distribute these among the guests, giving to each a plate, napkin, cup, and spoon, if necessary. The cups should be decorated with gypsy scenes and may be carried home as souvenirs.

After the drill and the refreshments the fortune-telling may be introduced if desired. Then for the latter part of the programme let a good reader give extracts from Barrie's "The Little Minister," either with or without illustrative tableaux. Some of the most effective scenes would be the riot at Thrums; the gypsy lass, Babbie, saving old Nanny from being taken to the poorhouse; the supper at Nanny's cottage; the gift of the bunch of holly in Caddam Wood, with Rob Dow watching from behind a tree; the quarrel at the well about the ring; the reconciliation; the appearance of Babbie at the manse with the lantern; the walk with the lantern and the meeting with the schoolmaster; Nanny trying to comfort Babbie before starting for church; Babbie and the little son of Rob Dow at the Standing Stone; the scene at the schoolhouse when Gavin is supposed to be dead; Babbie's confession of her identity; Lord Rintoul's inquiries at the schoolhouse; the kirk officers' search for the missing minister; the five scenes in the chapter "While the Ten o'Clock Bell was Ringing" (these should be given with the dialogue); the dominie's revelation to Gavin; Rob Dow's threats to his prisoner; her escape to the manse; the interview between Lord Rintoul and Babbie at the manse, between Babbie and Margaret, between Margaret and the precentor; Gavin on the island; the rescue by Rob Dow.

JUNIOR CHRISTIAN ENDEAVOR LINKS 155

Selections may be made from the list above for both the readings and the tableaux. If the readings alone are given, a greater latitude is of course possible than when they are illustrated.

JUNIOR CHRISTIAN ENDEAVOR LINKS

[This merits a word of special introduction because of its interesting history. It is an exercise given by the Junior Christian Endeavor society of the Odd Fellows' Orphanage of Philadelphia, Penn., under the direction of Mrs. L. A. Enoch, matron and superintendent, and Mr. George Hill, Junior Christian Endeavor instructor. While the idea and plan of the exercise were original with Mr. Hill, the matter for it, in part also original with him, was in part gleaned by him from various sources, which he has endeavored to credit in every instance where known; and the whole as thus arranged is contributed by Mr. Hill to this book's pages for the cause of Christian Endeavor and the boys and girls everywhere. — L. M. H.]

THE name "Links" was suggested because, as the Christian Endeavor movement had encircled the globe, so had the great order of Odd Fellows of which our society at the orphanage was a part, and a merging of the beautiful meanings of the two brought about this exercise. But the exercise is nevertheless adapted to the use of Christian Endeavor societies everywhere, from the small individual society to the large city union. It will be found very effective at rallies and conventions; in such instances a whole society or district instead of two or three children may represent each nation.

The color scheme originally used in the dresses of the children was based in part on the colors of the different degrees through which a member of the Order of Odd Fellows passes in advancing through the order, also on the colors of Christian Endeavor societies, our own (red and white) playing a conspicuous part. Each child held in his or her hand a large shield made of cardboard on which was tacked a large wooden link. Through the top of the link was a hole in which was placed at the outset a small silk flag of the country the child represented. After reciting or singing as the case might be, those representing that nation then retired and exchanged their flag for an American flag, remaining behind the scenes until it was time to make their appearance again in the grand finale.

The success of the exercise will depend largely on the one who trains the boys and girls and on the boys and girls themselves. A very large platform will be needed to give a proper setting to the exercise. The costumes of the various nations are not difficult to make. They may be copied from pictures or designed locally, as was the case in this instance.

The decorations of the room added greatly to the beautiful presentation. Flags of all nations were thus used, pictures, bunting and cheesecloth of different colors, and large shields with Christian Endeavor monograms pasted on them. Over the entrance to the platform were suspended two large American flags, while under these and extending to each side were the society's colors, red on one side and white on the other, through which the nations entered and departed. Suspended from the very centre was a board two feet square on which was a large Christian Endeavor monogram. As each nation retired, its flag was handed to the "consul," a boy who placed it in the Christian Endeavor monogram, which looked like this at the end of the exercise:

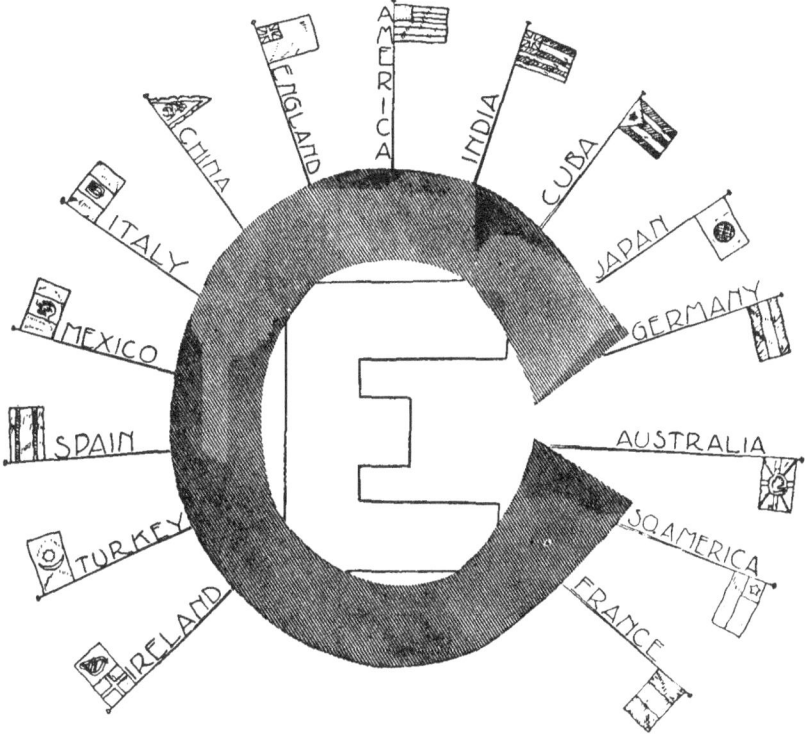

The shield held by each child was made of heavy cardboard and covered with glazed or colored paper to imitate as nearly as possible the flag of the country represented. On the back of the shield was a thick card strap so that the child could hold it, the hand being concealed. The links were sawed out of half-inch wood with a hole bored in through the top so that the little flag itself could be easily inserted and withdrawn. Each link before being tacked

158 ENJOYABLE ENTERTAINMENTS

on the face of the shield was wrapped in colored bunting. (Cheesecloth, muslin, or any soft material would do.) The same material was used in making the costumes worn by all the participants.

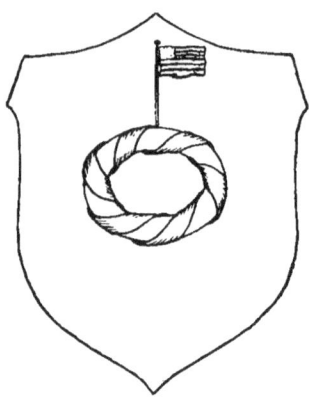

METHOD OF WRAPPING

OPENING CHORUS, "WELCOME SONG"[1]

The fragrance of lilies and roses,
    And violets hid in the wood,
The perfume of old-fashioned posies,
    We'd borrow them all if we could;
And gayly we'd take them and toss them
    For breezes to scatter at play,
And fling out a banner of blossom
    To welcome you, friends, here to-day.

We welcome you, welcome you, friends,
    With cheeriest carolling gay,
And praise to the Saviour of children,
    Who gave us this festival day.

---

[1] Tune from "The Junior Garden Exercise"; words from the Nashville, 1898, Junior Rally; both published by the United Society of Christian Endeavor, Boston, Mass.

O, sunny our faces and merry,
    And sunny our greeting and true,
Our faces all bright as a berry,
    Because they are welcoming you;
For happy the service of Jesus,
    And happy His children for aye;
He knows us, He hears us, He sees us,
    And He will be with us to-day.

During the singing of this song all the participants in the exercise are grouped on the platform in their usual dress, the small children in front, the larger ones in the rear. After the singing, all march to the rear with music accompaniment, boys to one side, girls to the opposite; retire and dress.

Recitation, "Greetings"[1]

Old Father Time has turned his glass;
    Another year has flown;
We come to greet each other here
    In old familiar tone.

Our Junior work will be our theme,
    The children still our song;
For, if the youth grow up aright,
    The nations will be strong.

Our Master gave a broad command,
    "Go, and all nations teach";
And henceforth friendship, love, and truth
    Men everywhere may preach,

---

[1] Adapted from "An Evening with the Juniors," United Society of Christian Endeavor, Boston, Mass.

And show by ministries of love
　The brotherhood of man;
Unselfish action best can prove
　The noble gospel plan.

A few strains of a march are played; and a boy and a girl enter, the boy representing the nation's consul and the girl the hostess. The consul takes a position under the large shield and Christian Endeavor monogram hanging in the centre. The hostess takes her position at one side of the platform. She is dressed in a white dress with red sash and red and white hair-ribbon, and holds in her left hand a Christian Endeavor shield made like this:

RED AND WHITE

The hostess now announces, in recitation [1]:

　The children are joyfully coming
　　From every land under the sun;
　While the tongues and the nations are many,
　　Our hearts and our wishes are one.

[1] From Nashville, 1898, exercise, United Society of Christian Endeavor, Boston, Mass.

JUNIOR CHRISTIAN ENDEAVOR LINKS

The hostess is then ready to receive the nations. As each nation is announced, its representatives appear, speak to the hostess, and in retiring from the stage pass their flag to the consul, who places it in the Christian Endeavor monogram. Then, while behind the scenes, they get the American flag (a small silk one), place it in their link, and wait until it is time to reappear in the finale. This is the procedure for all the nations, carried out through the whole exercise. Except where otherwise stated the platform is entirely clear of one nation before the next appears.

HOSTESS. Let us call the roll of the nations,
    And list what the children say;
Let us hear from the young crusaders
    Who are in the ranks to-day.

Impressive music, at the end of which a boy and a girl enter, representing England. The girl wears a red dress and red hair-ribbon, and carries a red shield on which is a green link and in the top a small silk English flag. The boy wears a red vest, hat, and suit of "John Bull," and carries a red shield on which is a pink link bearing an English flag. While they are approaching, they are thus introduced:

HOSTESS.
The children of England will greet you first,
    In blest Endeavor's name,
And for the Juniors of their land
    Their message now proclaim.

The boy and the girl stand together and the boy recites:

The boys and girls of England,
    O, who shall guide their feet?

O, who shall train and lead them
  Their country's needs to meet?
O blessed work, O sweet reward,
  To save these precious pearls —
To train for God, to guide and guard,
  Old England's boys and girls!

"And a little child shall lead them."

The girl recites:

The boys and girls of England,
  O, happy may they be!
The hope of home and country,
  The noble, good, and free.
With warm affection richly blessed,
  In virtue trained and truth,
May grace and mercy ever rest
  On all our cherished youth.

"And a little child shall lead them."

Both together recite:

The boys and girls of England,
  O, happy may they be!
The hope of home and country,
  The noble, good, and free.

They retire from the stage, passing their flags to the consul as they go.

HOSTESS. Next we have a representative from a country far away on the opposite side of the earth, China.

A boy enters dressed in a Chinese suit — blue trousers, yellow shirt, pink hat, and cue — and carries a yellow shield with a small Chinese flag inserted in a pink link. He takes his place on the side of the platform opposite where England stood and recites:

> Greetings from the country far across the sea!
> We bring our message now to thee.
> We come from China; dark and deep
> Pacific's rolling billows sweep
> 'Twixt your fair land and ours, where now
> Unnumbered millions blindly bow
> And prayers are heard and vows are paid
> To gods which their own hands have made.

We bring you Paul's message from the book of Philippians 1:9, "And this I pray, that your love may abound yet more and more in knowledge and in all judgment." [*Retires*]

HOSTESS. A representative from the sunny land of Italy.

A girl now appears, a black-haired little maid in a green skirt and red shirt-waist, a red and white shawl over her shoulder, with a red and green hair-ribbon. She carries a shield of red, white, and green, the colors of Italy, with an Italian flag in a green link.

Italy recites:

> And the Juniors from the land of Italy
>   Wish to send their message to you;
> They join in your glad endeavor
>   And try to be loyal and true.

"Whatsoever ye do, do it heartily as to the Lord, and not unto men." [*Retires*]

HOSTESS.
> Mexico comes in native dress;
>   Let not a sound be heard,
> But listen one and all, so still,
>   And hear her every word.

164 ENJOYABLE ENTERTAINMENTS

Enter Mexico, a girl with dark eyes, dark complexion, and black hair hanging loose, parted in the middle, clad in a yellow dress with black blouse, a purple sash around her waist hanging down nearly to the ground; beads on her head and arms. She carries a shield of the Mexican red,

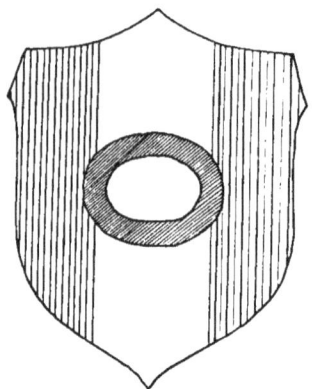

MEXICO — GREEN, WHITE, RED, AND BLUE

white, and green, with a blue link bearing a Mexican flag, and takes her place toward the right, leaving room for the next two nations (boys) to stand on each side of her. After the last of the three recites, all three retire together.

Mexico recites:

> I come from the land where the light and the darkness,
> The good and the evil, are ever at strife;
> O send to our people the gospel of Jesus
> That we too may find the way of ife.

"Not by might, nor by power, but by my spirit, saith the Lord."

HOSTESS. To Spain we look with gratitude,
Who sent Columbus here;

And may the Juniors from that land
The gospel message bear.

Spain appears, a boy wearing a suit trimmed with yellow and red, yellow sash, hat, etc. He carries a shield of

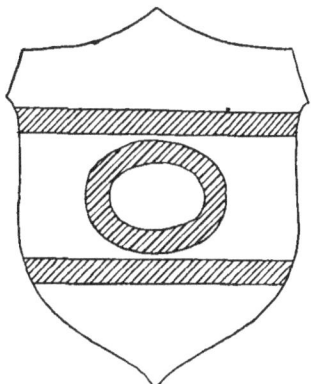

SPAIN — RED, YELLOW, AND PINK

yellow with red stripes across it and a Spanish flag in a pink link; he takes his place on the right of Mexico and recites:

In vain to Our Lady who sits queen of heaven
  We offer up prayers without ceasing;
We cannot forget that the Lord we must meet,
  And our terror is ever increasing.
If the Father of mercies has given a Book
  Which teaches the way of salvation,
Should not those who receive it make known the
    glad news
  And send it to every nation?

"In the midst of the street of it was there the tree of life, which bare twelve manner of fruits; and the leaves of the tree were for the healing of the nations." [*Remains on the right side of Mexico*]

ENJOYABLE ENTERTAINMENTS

Hostess. Now Turkey.

>Turkey sad and oft oppressed
> Has a message for us too;
> Speak out right loud so all can hear
> The golden rule from you.

Turkey appears, a boy wearing a red vest, sash, fez, and necktie, and carrying a red shield with a flag of Turkey inserted in a red link. He stands on the left of Mexico and recites:

> From the people who worship Mohammed
> We come with our message to-day,
> To thank you of Christian Endeavor
> For sending your gospel our way;
> Through the love you bore to the Master
> You have striven His will to heed,
> And have sent the glad, good tidings
> To the Turkish children in need.

"Whatsoever ye would that men should do to you, do ye even so to them."

Spain, Mexico, and Turkey now retire together, passing their flags to the consul, who places them in the Christian Endeavor monogram.

Hostess. From the Emerald Isle we greet you.

Immediately Ireland appears, a boy with red hair and freckles, wearing a green hat, vest, tie, and stockings, and carrying a green shield with a red link bearing an Irish flag. He takes his place on the extreme left of the platform, so that the next two nations will be able to stand on his right; this to correspond to the three preceding nations, who had been presented from the right side of the platform a few minutes before.

Ireland recites:

> *Sure* [emphatic] the strength of one child is nothing,
> But we'll gather in one strong band
> The strength of ten thousand Juniors
> For Endeavor throughout our land.

"If ye love me, keep my commandments."

Remains on the platform while the next two nations appear and recite.

HOSTESS. From France.

A boy appears wearing a yellow and purple vest, a white hat with red band, a red, white, and blue shield (the tricolor of France), with pink link bearing the French flag.

France recites:

> Through length and breadth of sunny France
> Is heard the gospel's truth,
> And in Endeavor's ranks now shine
> Her sunny-hearted youth.

"Exalt ye the Lord our God, and worship at His footstool."

HOSTESS. And from South America too

> They have come from across the great sea
> To bring their glad message to thee.

South America appears, a girl with a white dress, red blouse, red and white hair-ribbon, red and white shield, blue link, and flag of the Isthmus of Panama.

South America recites:

Not from the distant Orient I;
Our land lies 'neath your own dear sky,
And so from over the southern border
With message of greeting to thee we come.

"Our help is in the name of the Lord, who made heaven and earth."

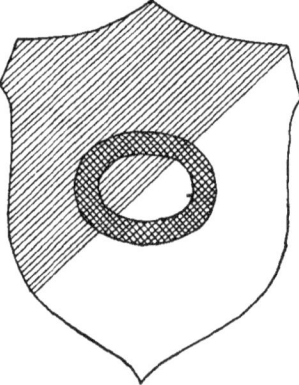

Isthmus of Panama (South America) — Red, White, and Blue

France, South America, and Ireland now retire together, giving their flags to the consul, who places them in the Christian Endeavor monogram.

Hostess. From far-off Australia a messenger now comes, who sings in sweetest lay.

Australia appears, a girl who can sing, wearing a green skirt, pink blouse, and pink and green hair-ribbon; she carries a shield of pink and green, with a pink and green link and as a flag the royal standard of Great Britain. She sings as a solo the song "Australia" in the Junior Rally exercise of Nashville, 1898, published by the United Society

JUNIOR CHRISTIAN ENDEAVOR LINKS 169

of Christian Endeavor, Boston, Mass. After singing, Australia recites:

From the southern climes we hail you with Christian Endeavor greetings. Your Master is ours and we are all His children.

"I was glad when they said unto me, Let us go into the house of the Lord." [*Retires*]

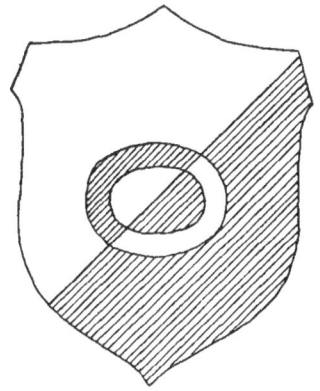

AUSTRALIA — GREEN AND PINK

HOSTESS.   And now the German Juniors come,
            Dressed as in days of old;
            So listen all attentively
            While their message sweet is told.

Three girls now appear dressed in German costumes of red skirts, black bodices over white blouses, hair in plaits down their backs, red and black hair-ribbons on the plaits. They carry shields of red, white, and black. The first girl's shield has a black link on it, the second a yellow link, and the third a purple, with a small German flag in each. Besides the hair-ribbon low down on the plait, the first girl wears on her head a red hair-ribbon, the second a white one, and the third a black one. They take their places on the left side of the platform.

The first girl recites:

> Italy, Mexico, and Spain
>   Came to answer to your call;
> Turkey, France, now Germany,
>   Come to greet you one and all.

"Fight the good fight of faith; lay hold on eternal life."

The second girl recites:

> We are Juniors from Germany,
>   And come from the Fatherland too;
> We come from across the Atlantic
>   To bring our message to you.

"Ye shall know the truth, and the truth shall make you free."

The third girl recites:

> Juniors, Juniors, happy Juniors,
>   What a blessed work you do!
> You have sent the news of Endeavor
>   To our distant nation too.

"Uphold me according to Thy word, that I may live."

All three girls now *chant* together Psalm 133, then retire, leaving their flags with the consul.

Hostess. And from Japan they come to-day,
  Dressed in the queerest way:
Attentive still we all must be
  To hear what they will say.

Enter three girls dressed in Japanese costume: figured material, flowing sleeves, "obi" sash, hair done up in knots with small fans, etc., stuck through. They take their places on the right of the platform when reciting. All three carry shields on which is the red ball of Japan. The first girl's shield has a black link on it, the second a yellow, the third a purple, all three links having small Japanese flags inserted.

The three girls recite together in opening:

"The Juniors of the Flowery Kingdom greet you in the Master's name."

One of the three then steps forward and recites:

JAPAN [1]

It was on the holy Lord's Day, dear and soul-reviving day,
That a fleet of seven warships cast anchor in Yeddo Bay;
'Twas a day that marked a crisis in the history of man,
For America was knocking at the closed door of Japan.
And the brave Commander Perry at the portal was to claim
Right of entrance and protection in his country's honored name.
On the capstan of his vessel were the stars and stripes [*show them*] outspread,
Flag of brotherhood and union, flag for which the brave have bled;
And upon the well-loved banner was the open Bible laid [*show a Bible*],
Book that tells of one great Father who has all races made.
Then the voice of praise and worship rose upon the Lord's Day calm,
Reverently the good commander read the joyous Hundredth Psalm.

[1] From "Recitations and Dialogues for Missionary Entertainments," compiled by Mattie Pounds, 152 East Market Street, Indianapolis, Ind.

And the brave notes of Old Hundred floated out across the bay,
Drifting dying in the distance on the waters far away.
Not a hostile gun was fired from the fleet or from the shore,
And to Christians' hymns of praises open swung the long-closed door.

In unison the three then recite Psalm 100 and retire.

HOSTESS.

> The girls of India in richest dress
> May now come forth to view;
> And, speaking, they will fail not to impress
> Their earnest message, too.

Four girls — a quartette of singers, representing the widows of India — appear, dressed as follows: The first girl all in white — white dress, white shawl over her head, white shield, white link. The second girl all in pink, the same arrangement; the third girl in blue; the fourth in red. All four links have English flags inserted.

The first girl recites:

"Why do the heathen rage, and the people imagine a vain thing?"

The second girl:

"The kings of the earth set themselves and the rulers take counsel together against the Lord and against His anointed, saying,"

The third girl:

"Let us break their bands asunder, and cast away their cords from us."

The fourth girl:

"He that sitteth in the heavens shall laugh; the Lord shall have them in derision."

All four in unison:

"Kiss the Son, lest he be angry and ye perish from the way when His wrath is kindled but a little. Blessed are all they that put their trust in Him."

The quartette then sing:

"OUR SUNSET SONG"[1]

Now o'er the waters [*point down*]
    Burns the crimson afterglow;
From a hundred temples [*point right*]
    Fades the day so slow [*point out*].
Where the palm-tree rises [*look to the left*],
    Telling of a foreign strand [*look to the right*],
Turn our hearts in sorrow [*hands on the heart*]
    For this stranger land.

Chorus

    India, sad India!
Let the dead years speak no more [*look down sadly*],
    India, sad India!
Open now thy door [*look up pleadingly*].

Far toward the sunset [*point to the right*]
    Lies a land to pilgrims dear,
But alone in dreaming
    Do its shores draw near [*poin down and wave the hand from left to right in a semicircle*].

[1] By Miss A. G. Frost. Arranged from "Juanita" by W. E. M. Hackman; in "Junior Builders' Songs," published by Miss Mattie Pounds, 152 East Market Street, Indianapolis, Ind.

> But the heart grows braver
> Looking toward that homeland shore [*look up, point out*]
> For the time is coming
> When the sea's no more [*point to the left and right*].

All four retire in the order given: white, pink, blue, red.

HOSTESS. The islands of the sea will be represented by a company of six Cuban patriots.

These are six boys who can sing, dressed in yellow khaki cloth suits and yellow hats on which are small Cuban flags. Each boy holds a shield of the Cuban colors, with

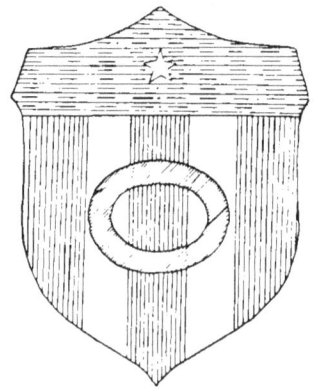

CUBA — RED, WHITE, BLUE, AND YELLOW

a small silk Cuban flag in the top of the link. The first boy (an orderly) has a red link, the second a white, the third a pink, the fourth (a bugler) a blue, the fifth a red, the sixth (the captain) a white.

After the hostess makes the announcement the bugler appears first, to music, sounds a call, and retires. Then the six patriots appear and give a drill and march, after which they form in a single column and recite as follows, each boy in turn stepping out and saluting the captain before reciting.

The first boy (orderly):

"The isles shall wait upon me, and on mine arm shall they trust."

The second boy:

> We bring you from our island home
> The children's greeting, "Yok-We-Kom."
> In southern seas our islands lie
> Beneath the burning tropic sky.

"Now are we the sons of God."

The third boy:

> Our people's thatched huts low and dark
> Nestle beneath the palms — and hark!
> Far on the reef the breakers roar,
> White wavelets meet the quiet shore.

"And it doth not yet appear what we shall be."

The fourth boy:

> We know God loves both you and me,
> And so He sent across the sea
> His messengers of joy and light
> To teach us what is pure and right.

"But we know that, when He shall appear."

The fifth boy:

> We pray, God bless the Christian ships
> And watch them as they sail afar,
> And bless each one whose loving heart
> Holds in God's ships his little part.

"We shall be like Him, for we shall see Him as He is."

176 ENJOYABLE ENTERTAINMENTS

The sixth boy (captain):

Yes, down in our Cuban isle we felt the heavenly breeze
Which wafted the glad tidings across the stormy seas;
We thank America for Christian Endeavor; her flag we will
  defend;
While the islands of the sea remain, Cuba will be her friend.

"The earth is the Lord's, and the fulness thereof; the world, and they that dwell therein; for He hath founded it upon the seas, and established it upon the floods."

This part of the exercise closes with another short drill, after which the six Cuban patriots take their places on the extreme rear of the platform, at the left side, facing the audience, in the following positions:

	Orderly			Captain	
White		Pink	Blue		Red

A march is now played, and all the nations previously appearing reappear and take the same positions as they did at first; only now each has a small silk American flag

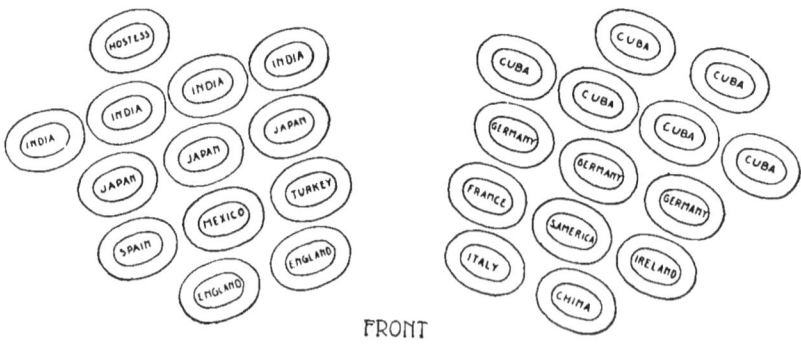
FRONT

in his or her link. They are grouped at this time as shown in the diagram, and remain so while the sextette sings [1]:

> There's a call that comes from Cuba,
>   Come and help us!
> The light of the gospel bring;
>   O come!
> Let us hear the joyful tidings of salvation;
> We thirst for the living spring.

All the nations then join in singing as follows:

> They shall gather from the east,
> They shall gather from the west,
>   With the patriarchs of old;
> And the ransomed shall return
> To the kingdoms of the blest
>   With their harps and crowns of gold.
>
> Let the distant isles be glad;
> Let them hail the Saviour's birth,
>   And the news of pardon free,
> Till the knowledge of the truth
> Shall extend to all the earth
>   As the waters o'er the sea.

HOSTESS. Here come the Junior Christian Endeavorers from all the other nations.

Eight Juniors appear (four boys and four girls) carrying shields alternately white and red, each shield with a link in the centre, an American flag inserted in the top of the link and a letter in the open centre of the link. The girls wear white dresses with red sashes. These eight Juniors

[1] Adapted from the Nashville, 1898, Christian Endeavor Rally, United Society of Christian Endeavor, Boston, Mass.

stand in the centre of the platform, placed so that their letters will spell the following:

      J U N I O R
         C   E

and recite in unison:

"Jesus said, Suffer the little children to come unto me, and forbid them not; for of such is the kingdom of heaven."

They remain standing in this position.

HOSTESS [*announces*]. Miss Columbia's Juniors!

To music (a patriotic air) three children appear, the first dressed all in red, the second in white, and the third in blue, each with a shield and link of the same color as the costume, the links bearing American flags. These march to the front of the platform, recite in unison, "God is love," and then take their stand immediately in the rear of the group forming the Junior C E.

A few strains of march music follow and a tiny tot makes her appearance (we used our three-year-old girl dressed in white with red sash, our Christian Endeavor colors) and marches (with guidance) to the centre of the platform at the front, taking a position in front of and between those having the letters C E, thus binding the two together and making the centre of the platform look like this:

    Red   White   Blue
   J U N I O R
     C   E
        X

The shield carried by the little one last appearing is quite distinctive. As originally arranged the shield had a

JUNIOR CHRISTIAN ENDEAVOR LINKS

white background with five red links, each having a letter in the centre and grouped thus:

[As the F. L. T. represents the motto of the Independent Order of Odd Fellows — Friendship, Love, Truth — some may prefer to substitute something else for this feature, though its significance is a beautiful and by no means inappropriate one as related to Christian Endeavor itself, with a word of explanation from the Hostess, thus:

> Our Christian Endeavor comrades
> In the gladness of their youth
> Now link the world in peaceful bonds
> Of Friendship, Love, and Truth.

Or, instead of any letters at all in this shield, let there be but one central link, and in it place a heart of gold, a symbol requiring no words of interpretation. — L. M. H.]

HOSTESS. And now the last, but not the least,
> In fond affection's chain
> These too would bring a message dear
> To all who've gathered here.

To the music of "The Star-Spangled Banner" Uncle Sam enters from one side and Miss Columbia from the other, both appropriately costumed, and amid waving of flags and strains of music, including the singing in full chorus of one verse of the above-named song, they take their places on opposite sides of the platform, in front, and each recites in turn. First, Uncle Sam, whose recitation is to be selected.

Miss Columbia recites:

America we represent, and all her children dear
Now bring their tribute to lay down with other nations here;
We greet you in the Master's name, and tell of union sweet
When all the nations of the world around God's throne shall meet.

Unto this land is given a privilege most rare;
A wealth of inspiration is hers to use and share;
The key to mighty problems of home and church and state
Is in this nation's keeping; God bids us work and wait.

If we will but unlock it, God's future fair and grand,
If we will plant His banner wherever people stand,
Our country, fully Christian and strong in Jesus' might,
Can take the world a captive, and lead it to the light.

The recitation closes with Psalm 67.

If no suitable selection for Uncle Sam is at hand, the recitation just given can be divided between the two, Miss Columbia perhaps giving the first stanza, Uncle Sam the second and third, and Miss Columbia closing with the psalm. Both then retire to the centre of the platform in the rear, under the Christian Endeavor monogram, and stand on a small raised platform, which should be quite high.

A large white cross, the long arm three feet high and the short arm two feet wide, is now placed on a pedestal or table on the centre of the platform, just in front of Miss Columbia and Uncle Sam, but not high enough to hide them. Red letters across the short arm form the word LOVE; at the foot of the cross are white lilies, and hanging on its top a wreath of red roses.

Enter a girl in a white dress, red sash, and red hair-ribbon, carrying a white shield with red letters also forming the word LOVE. She advances to the front of the platform and recites, addressing the nations [1]:

> I am Love, that gentle spirit;
> I am of a heavenly birth,
> But the cry of need has found me,
> And henceforth I dwell on earth.
>
> Take the cross [*pointing to it*], my gift of blessing;
> Bid it speak of Calvary;
> It shall conquer doubt and hatred,
> And the waiting world be free.
>
> Take the cross; no other token
> Can win a world from sin;
> Take the cross, and where it leads you,
> Quickly, gladly enter in.

"Come unto me, all ye that labor and are heavy laden, and I will give you rest."

All nations on the platform now recite in unison John 3:16. Then Love retires to the right rear of the platform, beside the hostess, facing the audience.

[1] From "The Conquering Cross," Fillmore Brothers, Cincinnati, Ohio.

At a signal all (except those in the centre and Uncle Sam and Miss Columbia, who will review the procession) form in a complete circle around the cross, make one complete revolution around it, singing while marching one verse of "Onward, Christian Soldiers." Then, keeping the circle still intact, all nations sing:

Chain of Love [1]

O chain of love that yet shall bind
The warring hearts of human kind!
This chain shall reach from hand to hand,
From life to life, from land to land.

Chorus

Around the cross the chain, the chain we raise,
And lift aloft our hymn and flags of praise,
  O chain of love, O wondrous chain,
  Sweet bondage of Messiah's reign!

O chain of love, O chain that draws
The minds of men to nobler laws;
Speed on the day, speed on the hour,
When all the world shall know its power. — *Cho.*

On the second line of the chorus raise shields and flags aloft and wave them.

Still in the same position around the cross all nations sing one verse of "Blest be the tie that binds," after which on a signal they march back to their original positions facing the audience, and as a finale sing the first and fourth verses of "America," in which the audience joins. The diagram

[1] Adapted from "The Conquering Cross," Fillmore Brothers, Cincinnati, Ohio.

JUNIOR CHRISTIAN ENDEAVOR LINKS 183

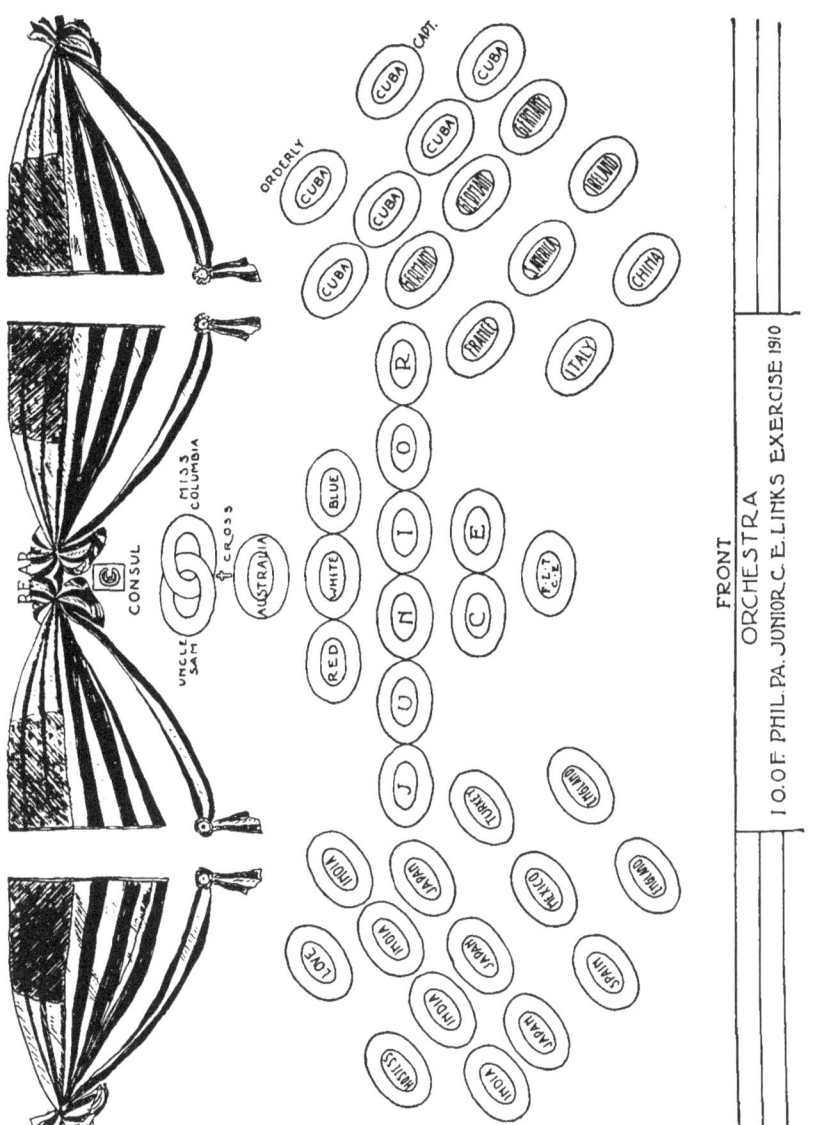

shows the positions of all on the platform at the conclusion of the exercise. A march or drill by the entire company follows, ending by their marching off the platform at the rear, the girls to one side, the boys to the other, the last one to leave the platform being the consul, who politely bows and retires.

[For this final march some of the movements described elsewhere in these pages under the title of "A Simple March," especially the "mainspring" or "winding" portion, would be effective, as would also some portions of the drill given in the exercise "The Building of the Church." — L. M. H.]

www.ingramcontent.com/pod-product-compliance
Lightning Source LLC
Chambersburg PA
CBHW031349040426
42444CB00005B/247